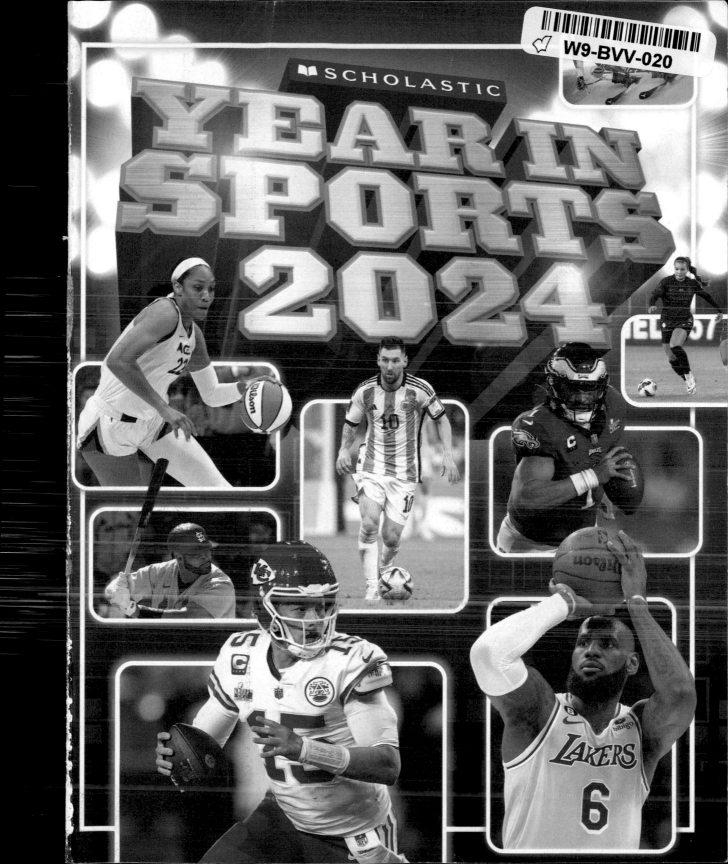

SCHOLASTIC

YEAR IN SPORTS 2024

Copyright © 2024 by Shoreline Publishing Group LLC

All rights reserved. Published by Scholastic Inc., *Publishers since 1920*. SCHOLASTIC and associated logos are trademarks and/or registered trademarks of Scholastic Inc.

No part of this publication may be reproduced, stored in a retrieval system, or transmitted in any form or by any means, electronic, mechanical, photocopying, recording, or otherwise, without written permission of the publisher. For information regarding permission, write to Scholastic Inc., Attention: Permissions Department, 557 Broadway, New York, NY, 10012.

ISBN 978-1-339-01132-5

10 9 8 7 6 5 4 3 2 1   24 25 26 27 28

Printed in the U.S.A.   40
First edition, January 2024

Produced by Shoreline Publishing Group LLC

Due to the publication date, records, results, and statistics are current as of mid-August 2023.

UNAUTHORIZED: This book is not sponsored by or affiliated with the athletes, teams, or anyone involved with them.

Contents

Whew! What a Year!

Timeout! Are you as hot and sweaty as we are? What a wild year in sports this has been! We're worn out from running all over the globe to watch so much exciting action on fields, rinks, courts, diamonds, mountains, tracks, and more! We need a break! Good thing it's time to sit down and read another edition of the YEAR IN SPORTS!

Our wild ride through 365 days of sports began with **Lionel Messi** leading Argentina to his first World Cup championship. He later made headlines by joining Miami of Major League Soccer (MLS)! Then the Las Vegas Aces won their first WNBA championship. **Sophia Smith** led the Portland Thorns to the top in the National Women's Soccer League. MLS 2022 ended with one of the best games in the league's history, as LAFC snuck ahead of the Philadelphia Union. Before the soccer ball stopped bouncing, the Houston Astros were knocking off the surprising Philadelphia Phillies in the World Series.

Out on the track, the top racing series wrapped up their high-speed action. **Max Verstappen** repeated as Formula 1 champ. NASCAR's **Joey Logano** won his second title, while **Will Power** became a two-time champ in IndyCar.

Jumping onto the stage next was college football, where fans of the Georgia Bulldogs got to cheer the loudest as their team repeated as the national champs. Football fans then turned their eyes to the National Football League,

Georgia's Stetson Bennett with the top trophy.

LSU whoops it up as national champs!

which had a super-exciting postseason. Super Bowl LVII turned out to be one of the best ever! **Patrick Mahomes** led a late drive to a winning field goal over a tough and gutsy Philadelphia Eagles team led by **Jalen Hurts**.

Are you tired yet? There's so much more to come!

LSU won its first women's college basketball title. The Vegas Golden Knights skated to the Stanley Cup championship, while the Toronto Six won the women's Premier Hockey Federation title. The Denver Nuggets won their first NBA championship as the summer heated up.

Catch your breath, because the sports kept coming!

Summer saw the end of other top soccer leagues, plus an historic "triple" by Manchester City in England, while Barcelona won another women's Champions League title. The year capped off with the most successful Women's World Cup ever. The event in Australia and New Zealand attracted a record audience while showcasing some of the best women's soccer yet. The United States team was disappointed in its result, but fans of Spain ended up cheering the loudest as their team beat England 1-0.

During the year, a big number of all-time heroes retired; check out a special salute to them on page 24. And then take a break with a big glass of lemonade and this book. You've earned a rest!

TOP 10 MOMENTS IN SPORTS

You're about to dive into page after page of memorable and incredible sports events. Here's a preview of what we think were the biggest and best from the 2022–23 sports year.

10 **A TRULY CLASSIC CLASSIC** *The World Baseball Classic had been held four times before 2023. But the 2023 event was the biggest and best yet! Teams from around the world battled to reach the finals, which ended up as Japan vs. the United States. Huge crowds packed stadiums, and millions watched around the world on TV. The final out was like a movie script. Japan's megastar* **Shohei Ohtani** *struck out LA Angels teammate* **Mike Trout** *to win Japan's third WBC.*

9 PURPLE POWER! *The fifth time was a charm for the LSU Tigers. The team had reached the NCAA championship game five times, but had not cut down the nets. The wait ended in April when **Angel Reese** (in purple) powered her team to the school's first title. The Tigers roared loudest in the end, knocking off Iowa and its own superstar, **Caitlin Clark**, 102-85.*

8 **OF COURSE HE DID!** *Leave it to the best and most magical soccer player ever to create yet another memory. In his first game with Inter Miami in Major League Soccer in 2023,* **Lionel Messi** *steered in a free kick in the final minute to beat Cruz Azul 2-1. It was a fairy-tale beginning to his time in the United States. What other tricks does Magic Messi have in store for us?*

7 **WHAT A GAME!** *Major League Soccer ended the 2022 season with a major-league MLS Cup game. It was an instant classic, featuring last-second goals, incredible saves, world superstars, and the league's two best teams: LAFC and Philadelphia Union. Both teams scored in overtime, including LAFC's **Gareth Bale** on a shocking header. The penalty-kick hero turned out to be LAFC's backup goalie, **John McCarthy**, who led his team to its first MLS title.*

6 A NEW NUMBER ONE

*LeBron James has been aiming for the top since he joined the NBA as a teenager in 2003. He has led three teams to NBA championships and earned countless trophies and awards. As he scored point after point for 20 seasons, he was aiming at the all-time scoring record, too. On February 7, 2023, he got it, topping the mark of 38,387 set by **Kareem Abdul-Jabbar**. The player known as "The King" is now the King of Scoring.*

5 **A SUPER SUPER BOWL!** *Fans enjoyed a real treat at the end of the 2022 NFL season. The Super Bowl was really, truly super! Kansas City won its second title under* **Patrick Mahomes**, *defeating the Philadelphia Eagles 38-35. The Eagles made it a real battle. QB* **Jalen Hurts** *led his team to a tying score late in the game. Then Mahomes had to drive for a game-winning field goal!*

NO. 1 ON THE SNOW *The World Cup of skiing—a series of races around the world—began way back in 1966. In 2023, a new all-time champion was crowned when American skier* **Mikaela Shiffrin** *won her 87th World Cup race. She set the mark with a slalom win in Sweden, which was the home of the previous record holder,* **Ingemar Stenmark***.*

TWO NEW CHAMPS

3 Both pro basketball leagues in the US had new champions. In 2022, the Las Vegas Aces, led by superstar **A'Ja Wilson** (below right), won their first WNBA crown. The Aces needed four games to defeat the Connecticut Sun. In the 2023 NBA Finals, the Denver Nuggets won their first title, too. Two-time NBA MVP **Nikola Jokić** (top, with daughter Ognjena) was the dominant player, leading his team to a five-game win over the Miami Heat.

2 **¡VIVA LAS CAMPEONAS!** Spain's **Olga Carmona** celebrates after scoring the only goal in the Women's World Cup (WWC) championship game. Spain won its first WWC 1-0 over England, wrapping up the most successful and best-played WWC ever. While fans of the US Women's National Team were disappointed, soccer fans enjoyed fast-moving, action-packed games from the best players in the world. Read all about the whole tournament on page 16.

1

MESSI . . . FINALLY! *Lionel Messi* had won just about everything you can win in world soccer. He was a seven-time World Player of the Year, a South American champion with Argentina, and a Champions League winner with Barcelona. But he and Argentina had failed in four other tries at the biggest prize—the World Cup. In 2022, Messi finally broke through. In one of the best final matches ever, France and Argentina tied 3-3, and Argentina won in penalty kicks. Messi was named the tournament's top player, but his favorite prize was the World Cup trophy.

CELEBRATE!

Spain's team danced in the flying confetti as they raised the Women's World Cup trophy for the first time. The team's 1-0 defeat of England capped off an amazing WWC tournament in Australia and New Zealand. New heroes were discovered, and people around the world watched some very exciting soccer. Read on to find out how Spain made it to the top!

Nearly 2 million people attended the Women's World Cup, setting a new all-time record.

2023 Women's World Cup

American fans didn't get their wish. Women's soccer fans did. The United States could not defend its Women's World Cup (WWC) title, but other great teams rose up in a super tournament held in Australia and New Zealand.

It was August 2023, but it was winter Down Under. Fans didn't care, bundling up to set a new attendance record. By the quarterfinals, more than 1.7 million people had gone to games. Attendance reached a new record at 1.975 million after the final.

On the way to that game, fans enjoyed some tremendous and exciting soccer . . . and some big upsets! This WWC had 32 teams, up from 24 in 2019. Eight teams were making their WWC debuts. Some experts wondered if that would make things better for top-ranked teams. Would they have more "easy" games against lower-ranked teams? As fans saw, that was not the case. Top teams from Europe had surprising results against teams from South America, the Caribbean, and Africa.

Three African teams made it through to the round of 16 for the first time. South Africa got a goal in injury time of its final game to send Italy home and earn its first round-of-16 spot. Nigeria played very well in earning a spot, including a big win over Canada. Morocco was the third, beating Colombia to earn its place. It was the first Arab country to even *win* a WWC game when it topped South Korea 1-0. In that game, **Nouhaila Benzina** was the first woman to play in a WWC while wearing a hijab. Morocco and Colombia teamed up to knock out world No. 2 Germany.

Jamaica had money troubles off the field

Marta (right) to Shaw: You're next!

Benzina and Morocco made headlines.

that almost kept the team from coming. But they made the trip and advanced for the first time. In its first game, it tied France, one of the world's top teams, 0-0. In its second, it got its first WWC win when it beat Panama. Then in its third game, another 0-0 tie with Brazil, it put an end to the greatest career in women's soccer. **Marta** had played in a record five WWCs and is the all-time leading WWC scorer with 17 goals. After the game, she congratulated Jamaica forward **Bunny Shaw**, who told Marta that she had been her inspiration growing up.

While the favored US team went out in the round of 16 (see page 22), Australia's loyal fans saw their team advance to the semifinals. And when Japan lost to Sweden, that meant that there would be a first-time champion in the WWC for the first time since Japan won in 2011.

The most successful WWC ever ended with two exciting semifinals and an historic final that capped off a fantastic tournament.

First Round Highlights

Eight groups of four teams each battled to send countries into the knockout round. The top two teams from each group made it. Most top-ranked teams went through, but there were surprises!

Catalina Usme (left) led Colombia to the upset.

Home Team Shockers! Cohost New Zealand thrilled its fans in Auckland by winning its first-ever WWC game. Hannah Wilkinson scored the game's only goal as the Football Ferns shocked Norway. Unfortunately for the home fans, New Zealand was upset 1-0 in its next game by the Philippines, who earned their own first-ever WWC victory. New Zealand then tied Switzerland 0-0 and was out of

the tournament. Australia, the other cohost, blasted past Canada 4-0 to move on to the knockout round.

Surprises at the Top: Three highly ranked teams had to survive first-game surprises in order to advance. England barely beat Haiti 1-0. France tied Jamaica 0-0, a game they were expected to win easily. A big win over Brazil gave France a spot in the knockouts. Nigeria held Canada to a surprise 0-0 tie. A big play was Nigeria goalie Chiamaka Nnadozie stopping a penalty kick by Christine Sinclair, who has scored more international goals than any player in soccer history! Nigeria ended up earning a spot in the final 16.

Rising Powers: Japan and Spain were among the first teams to move to the second round. Both put up big victories with high scores. Would they be the newest teams to challenge the US at the top?

Shocker! Germany is one of the top-ranked teams in the world. But when it faced No. 25–ranked Colombia, the rankings didn't matter. Germany tied the game 1-1 in the 89th minute. But the Colombians kept battling. In extra time, just a minute from the end, Manuela Vanegas knocked in a header to give Colombia a 2-1 win and the biggest upset of the first round of the tournament. Then South Korea tied Germany 0-0 and sent them home early!

Horan (#10 above and below) rose up above the Dutch defense to score a game-tying goal.

US First-Round Games

US 3, Vietnam 0

Sophia Smith emerged as an early-tournament star. She scored two goals and had the assist on **Lindsey Horan**'s second-half score. The US expected to score more, but Vietnam's goalie, **Trần Thị Kim Thanh**, made many excellent saves. She even stopped **Alex Morgan**'s penalty-kick attempt!

US 1, Netherlands 1

The US fell behind for the first time in a World Cup game since 2011. **Jill Roord** scored from the top of the penalty box in the 17th minute. But in the second half, US captain Horan knocked in a header on a corner kick. The US had lots more shots in the game but could not crack the Dutch defense.

US 0, Portugal 0

By the width of a soccer goalpost, the US squeaked into the knockout round. The American team managed only a few shots, while Portugal proved to be much tougher than expected. In the 91st minute, Portugal's **Ana Capeta** smacked a shot that bounced off the goalpost. If it had gone in, the US would have gone home! A narrow escape!

Knockout Rounds!

Round of 16 Winners
✱ Spain ✱ Netherlands ✱ Japan ✱ Australia
✱ England ✱ France ✱ Colombia ✱ Sweden

Quarterfinals
➤ Spain scored late in extra time to beat the Netherlands 2-1.
➤ After beating the US, Sweden stopped Japan's powerful attack to win 2-1.
➤ Australia outlasted France 7-6 in a long penalty-kick shootout to advance.
➤ England rallied after an early Colombia goal to win 2-1.

Semifinals
Spain 2, Sweden 1
In one of the most thrilling games of the tournament, Spain scored twice in the last ten minutes and headed to its first-ever final. Spain went ahead in the 81st minute, but Sweden tied it in the 87th. Then a fantastic long-range strike by **Olga Carmona** put Spain back on top to stay.

England 3, Australia 1
The hometown team fell short, while England earned its first trip to the final. A goal by Aussie star **Sam Kerr** tied the game in the second half. Then England's **Lauren Hemp** slipped in a go-ahead goal.

US Goes Home . . . By a Millimeter
The US lost to Sweden in penalty kicks after tying 0-0 after 120 minutes. The final Swedish PK just barely made it across the line, but it was enough to send the US home before the semifinals for the first time ever. Three US players missed PKs as well, a disappointing end to what many fans hoped would be a three-peat.

This long goal by Kerr (in yellow) gave Australian fans a reason to cheer . . . for a while.

Olga Carmona is about to blast this shot into the far side of the English net.

¡VIVA ESPAÑA!

With a display of really beautiful soccer, Spain won its first Women's World Cup, defeating England 1-0. The Spanish players performed with joy and some real dazzle. They made lots of quick, short passes; used long dribbling runs; and showed how the game can be exciting all the time. England played well but just could not match the Spanish team's speed and ball control. England goalie **Mary Earps** did make a huge penalty-kick save, but her teammates never found the back of the net.

Spain's **Olga Carmona** had the game's only goal. In the first half, playing left back, she followed the offense on an attack. Carmona raced to a pass on the left side of the penalty area and slammed a left-footed shot that slid along the grass into the far corner of the net past Earps. England had some chances, but Spain's defense held strong. Even when 13 minutes of extra time were added due to injuries and subs, Spain was able to keep England from scoring.

The game wrapped up the best and most successful WWC in history!

2023 WWC AWARDS

Golden Ball (BEST PLAYER)
Aitana **BONMATÍ**, Spain

Golden Boot (TOP SCORER)
Hinata **MIYAZAWA**, Japan

Golden Gloves (TOP GOALIE)
Mary **EARPS**, England

Top Young Player
Salma **PARALLUELO**, Spain

SO LONG...AND THANKS!

A long time from now, you'll be able to tell your kids that you saw these sports superstars in action. They all retired in the past year, but they'll be remembered forever.

⭐ SERENA WILLIAMS

Along with her sister Venus, Serena changed tennis as one of the first Black superstars. But after Serena kept winning and winning, she became so much more than that. Her incredible career included 23 Grand Slam singles titles, the second-most all-time. She also teamed with Venus to win 14 Grand Slam doubles titles. They also won three Olympic gold medals together, with Serena winning the singles title as well in 2012. With grace, power, and a fiery spirit, Serena will be remembered as one of the greatest ever in women's sports.

TOM BRADY

He was a superstar probably before you were born. And he was a superstar for your whole life, too. No one has been more successful in the NFL than Tom. His seven Super Bowl championships are the most ever, as are his five Super Bowl MVP trophies. He stands atop the list for most career TD passes (649), passing yards (89,214), and completions (7,753). Not only did he lead the Patriots to six Super Bowl wins, but at the age of 43, he led the Buccaneers to another one. Tom Brady = GOAT.

⭐ ALBERT PUJOLS

There are certain numbers in baseball that just mean more than others. One of them is 700. Only four out of the more than 23,000 Major League players in history have that many homers. In 2022, Albert Pujols became the fourth as he wrapped up his amazing career. Albert was a dominating slugger, with three MVPs in the 2000s. In fact, in eight out of nine seasons from 2002 through 2010, he finished in the top three in MVP votes. He was the rare player who could hit for average and with great power. Fans were thrilled as he chased 700 in his final burst of power (he reached 703), and his smile will be remembered as much as his swing.

★ SUE BIRD

The WNBA said goodbye to a legend in 2022. Four-time champion Sue Bird flew off into the sunset as one of the greatest women's players ever. She led the Seattle Storm to four championships, the first in 2004 and the last 16 years later in 2020. Sue racked up more games and minutes played than any other WNBA player, showing off fantastic passing skills and clutch shooting. All-time, she's first in assists, third in steals, and second in three-point baskets. Wearing the red, white, and blue, Sue also won five Olympic gold medals—another feather in her cap!

★ SYLVIA FOWLES

Basketball players miss about half their shots, and when that happened in the WNBA, Sylvia Fowles was there more often than anyone else. She retired after a 15-year, eight-All-Star Game career as the league's all-time best rebounder. Sylvia is not all about boards, either—her .599 career field-goal percentage is also tops all-time. Along with two WNBA titles (with the Minnesota Lynx in 2015 and 2017), she helped bring four Olympic gold medals home to the US. She can add those to her trophy shelf, which also includes a pair of Finals MVP awards, the 2017 WNBA MVP, and four Defensive Player of the Year honors.

★ROGER FEDERER

For a while, no one had won more men's Grand Slam singles titles than Roger Federer. While his career total of 20 has since been passed, the Swiss star leaves the sport as one of the all-time legends. During his 24-year career, he was No. 1 in the world for more than 300 weeks and won more than 100 singles championships. His first major title came at the 2003 Wimbledon tournament. He won his last at the 2018 Australian Open. His battles with fellow legend Rafael Nadal will be talked about for decades. Don't worry about Roger, though. Even without playing, he can still make millions from being in commercials!

★ ALLYSON FELIX

Careers in track and field are often about as long as the races themselves. That's what makes Allyson Felix so remarkable. As a 200- and 400-meter racer, she was one of the top runners in the world for 20 years, winning a women's record 11 medals over five Olympic Games. Seven of those were gold medals, including her first in 2008. At the 2022 World Championships, she added another record with 20 total medals. Allyson has been able to use her fame as a runner to speak up for social justice and equal rights, so don't think you've heard the last from this champion.

★ J.J. WATT

Only three players have been the NFL Defensive Player of the Year three times. The powerful pass-rushing J.J. Watt was the second, winning his third in 2015. That year, he led the NFL in sacks for the second time with 17.5. His career best of 20.5 came in his second season, 2012 (he did it again in 2014!). Though he battled injuries later in his career, Watt was an unstoppable force when healthy. If he couldn't reach the QB, he earned his "J.J. Swat" nickname by knocking down passes. Now he can watch younger brother T.J., a Pittsburgh Steelers pass-rusher, aim at his records.

AWESOME ALBERT

By the age of 42, most athletes are watching games from home. Not Albert Pujols. The slugging first baseman returned to the St. Louis Cardinals for a final season in 2022 after almost 10 years with the Angels. Pujols then thrilled all of baseball as he powered up for a tremendous last month. He hit 7 homers after Labor Day, including this one against the Dodgers for No. 700 of his career. He retired with 703 homers, fourth-most of all time.

MLB 2022

As the 2022 MLB season began (a week late due to some contract issues between players and owners), fans and players had a few new things to watch. First, the designated hitter in all games—AL and NL—was permanently used for the first time. The rule had been put in place during the 2020 COVID season, but by 2022, pitchers were done hitting for good. Perhaps that gave pitchers a chance to practice using the new PitchCom system that was in place for 2022. The system included touchpads on catchers' wrists and mini speakers in pitchers' hats. The new communication plan was designed to cut down on sign-stealing and perhaps speed up games.

The changes were not just on the field. For the first time, 12 teams would make the playoffs, including two teams that would earn byes for having the top record in their league. Opening up the playoffs added more excitement to the end of the season and wound up helping a surprise team reach the World Series.

Once the season began, the New York Yankees were having the most success. They started off 39–15, their best beginning to a season in 21 years. The Dodgers were not far behind; they were 33–16 by the end of May. Both those teams made the playoffs, of course, but neither won the World Series!

In Anaheim, the amazing **Shohei Ohtani** of the Angels continued one of the biggest stories in sports. After winning the AL MVP in 2021 as the best two-way player since **Babe Ruth**, Ohtani was actually almost better in 2022! He ended up with a higher batting average and another 34 homers, while improving to a 15–9 record and a 2.33 ERA. Other MLB pitchers had some incredible stats in 2022. Mets closer **Edwin Díaz** averaged 17 strikeouts per 9 innings! White Sox starter **Dylan Cease** put together a streak of 14

Shohei Ohtani

2022 FINAL MLB STANDINGS

AL EAST		AL CENTRAL		AL WEST	
Yankees	99–63	Guardians	92–70	Astros	106–56
Blue Jays	92–70	White Sox	81–81	Mariners	90–72
Rays	86–76	Twins	78–84	Angels	73–89
Orioles	83–79	Tigers	66–96	Rangers	68–94
Red Sox	78–84	Royals	65–97	Athletics	60–102

NL EAST		NL CENTRAL		NL WEST	
Braves	101–61	Cardinals	93–69	Dodgers	111–51
Mets	101–61	Brewers	86–76	Padres	89–73
Phillies	87–75	Cubs	74–88	Giants	81–81
Marlins	69–93	Reds	62–100	Diamondbacks	74–88
Nationals	55–107	Pirates	62–100	Rockies	68–94

games allowing one earned run or fewer. At 39, **Justin Verlander** returned from missing a whole year after arm surgery to lead MLB with a 1.75 ERA. He led the AL with 18 wins and won his third Cy Young Award. Overall, MLB pitchers threw more than 3,300 pitches at 100-miles-per-hour or more, the most ever in one season. Performances like that were a big reason that, as a group, big-league hitters averaged only .243, the lowest in more than 50 years!

The Baltimore Orioles had the biggest one-season turnaround, going from only 52 wins in 2021 to 83 in 2022. They were the first team ever to go from 110 losses to a record of better than even a year later. With young stars like **Adley Rutschman**, they could be a team to watch.

Speaking of young players, Atlanta rookie pitcher **Spencer Strider** was the first player ever with 200 Ks and fewer than 100 hits allowed in his first season. Both **Julio Rodríguez** and **Bobby Witt Jr.** had rare 20 (HR)–20 (SB) seasons.

The added playoff spots meant late division races. The defending-champion Atlanta Braves had a huge rally. They were seven games behind the Mets on August 10 but charged back. They swept a big end-of-season series over New York and wound up winning the NL East. Meanwhile, the Seattle Mariners had a great season, earning their first playoff spot in 21 seasons and ending baseball's longest postseason drought.

"Phinally," the Philadelphia Phillies were the last team to clinch a spot in the expanded playoffs. Then they made the most of their postseason run, as you'll see starting on page 38.

Edwin Díaz

2022 Diamond Notes

Perfect in Japan!:

A perfect game is incredible no matter what country it's thrown in. **Rōki Sasaki** tossed a perfecto for the Chiba Lotte Marines from Japan's pro baseball. It was the first one there since 1994, and Sasaki made it even better by striking out 19 Orix Buffaloes, tying a league record. Thirteen of those Ks came in a row, setting a record.

What a Start!:

Guardians OF **Steven Kwan** began his rookie season in record-setting fashion. He reached base 18 times in his first five MLB games, the most ever. Heck, he did even better than that. He didn't swing and miss on *any* of the first 116 pitches he saw in the bigs! He was hitting .354 by the end of April. Kwan ended up leading the Guardians with a .298 average, won the Gold Glove for his outfield defense, and finished third in the AL Rookie of the Year voting.

20 Ks:

Houston's **Framber Valdez** struck out 13 Angels in his six innings, and Astros relievers kept the Ks coming. When **Ryan Pressly** struck out the side in the ninth, Houston ended with an MLB-record-tying 20 strikeouts in the game.

Another Kind of Perfect:

In a perfect game, a pitcher doesn't allow any base runners. In an "immaculate inning,"

ALL RISE!

Aaron Judge had one of the most amazing seasons in baseball history in 2022. Already the record holder for homers by a rookie (52 in 2017), he broke **Roger Maris**'s AL record with his 62nd homer in the season's second-to-last game. Judge also led the AL with 131 RBI and came within .005 batting-average points of winning the Triple Crown, too! Judge won the Hank Aaron, Silver Slugger, and AL MVP Awards and a place in Yankees history.

a pitcher doesn't throw a ball. Angels pitcher **Reid Detmers** threw such an inning—nine pitches, nine strikes, three outs—against the Texas Rangers. Incredibly, it was the third time Texas had gone down 1-2-3 like that. It has only happened two other times to the rest of the league!

Super Streak:
In a September game against the Pirates, Mets ace **Jacob deGrom** set an all-time record with his 40th straight start allowing three runs or fewer. You have to track back to the 1913–14 seasons and a fellow named **Jim Scott** to find a pitcher whose streak of 39 DeGrom topped. DeGrom switched to the Texas Rangers for the 2023 season.

Soto Swap:
There are trades . . . and then there are TRADES! Just before the trade deadline in July, the Washington Nationals sent megastar **Juan Soto** to the San Diego Padres for six players. Experts called it one of the biggest trades ever, especially for a player with as much success and potential as Soto. Baseball writer Jayson Stark wrote, "No player like Juan Soto has ever been traded at any trade deadline. Ever. Period."

¡Viva Tampa Bay!:
On September 15, MLB honored the memory of the great Puerto Rican star **Roberto Clemente**. The Tampa Bay Rays went one further, starting players from Spanish-speaking countries at all nine positions, a baseball first. Colombia, Cuba, the Dominican Republic, Mexico, and Venezuela were all represented. The players all wore Clemente's No. 21, and we're sure he would have been pleased with Tampa's 11-0 win!

Steven Kwan,
Cleveland
Guardians

2022 MLB Playoffs

Houston's **Jeremy Peña** hit a homer in the 18th inning for the win (the 17-inning scoreless streak was the longest ever, breaking a week-old record; see box at right!). It also tied for the longest playoff game ever, innings-wise.

Houston rookie hero Jeremy Peña

NL Divisional Playoffs

Philadelphia 3, Atlanta 1
Surprisingly, the Phillies sent the World Series champs home early. **J.T. Realmuto** had the first inside-the-park homer by a catcher in MLB playoff history, while **Brandon Marsh** smacked a three-run homer as the Phils won Game 4, 8-3.

San Diego 3, LA Dodgers 1
The Dodgers won 111 games but couldn't seem to hit in this series. They were sent

AL Divisional Playoffs

NY Yankees 3, Cleveland 2
Homers from sluggers **Aaron Judge** and **Giancarlo Stanton** sealed a Game 5 win and the series for the Yankees. Cleveland had made it tough, forcing the Yankees to win Game 4 as well, thanks to ace starter **Gerrit Cole**.

Houston 3, Seattle 0
The Mariners' playoff run ended quickly with a sweep by the powerful Astros. The clinching game took a bit longer, though.

Hader was throwing heaters!

WILD CARD GAMES

AMERICAN LEAGUE

Cleveland 2, Tampa Bay 0
In the 15th inning of Game 2, the Guardians got a game- and series-winning homer from **Oscar González** (*right*) to sweep Tampa Bay. It was the only run of the game, which was, for a few days, the longest scoreless contest in playoff history.

Seattle 2, Toronto 0
The Mariners earned their first playoff spot since 2001 and made the most of it. They upset the Blue Jays, thanks to a big seven-run comeback in the clincher to win 10-9. It was the biggest comeback to win a series in postseason history.

NATIONAL LEAGUE

Philadelphia 2, St. Louis 0
The Phillies only won 87 games, but they earned the final NL playoff spot. In defeating the Cardinals, they

ended the career of the great **Albert Pujols** (page 33) and showed off the home run power of **Bryce Harper**.

San Diego 2, NY Mets 1
The Padres shocked the Mets with four homers off ace **Max Scherzer** in Game 1. After the Mets rallied with a Game 2 win, San Diego's **Joe Musgrove** pitched a gem in Game 3 to lead the way to a 6-0 series clincher.

home in a shocking upset by the Padres, who had finished 22 games behind the Dodgers. San Diego won the clincher 5-3 at home. **Josh Hader** struck out three Dodgers superstars—**Mookie Betts**, **Trea Turner**, and **Freddie Freeman**—to end the game.

ALCS

Houston 4, NY Yankees 0
The Astros continued to roll, sweeping the Yankees for their seventh straight postseason win. In the clinching game, ALCS MVP Peña smacked a three-run

homer and the Astros came from behind twice to win 6-5. It will be Houston's fourth World Series appearance since 2017.

NLCS

Philadelphia 4, San Diego 1
Bryce Harper signed a 13-year contract with the Phillies in 2019. He proved to be a good choice, as he smacked a go-ahead two-run homer to clinch a 4-3 Game 5 win over the Padres. The Phillies became the first team ever to finish third in their division and make it to the World Series.

2022 World Series

GAME 1 Philadelphia 6, Houston 5
The Phillies rallied from being five runs behind to surprise the Astros in Houston. **Kyle Tucker** had given the home team a lead with 2 homers and 4 RBI by the third inning. The computers said the Phillies' chances of winning were only 7 out of 100. But the Astros' ace, **Justin Verlander**, could not hold the lead. Philly tied the game in the fifth inning on a double by **J.T. Realmuto**. The Phillies bullpen then held the Astros scoreless for almost five innings, until a 10th-inning homer by Realmuto gave the Phillies the winning run.

Four pitchers and a catcher were great!

GAME 2 Houston 5, Philadelphia 2
The Astros again jumped out to a 5-0 lead, but this time they held on, thanks to a great start by **Framber Valdez**. Houston's star second baseman, **José Altuve**, had been struggling, hitting less than .150 in the postseason, before getting three hits in this game. His leadoff double led to three runs in the first and the Astros stayed in control after that.

Brandon Marsh homered for Philly in Game 3.

GAME 3 Philadelphia 7, Houston 0
The Phillies brought the lumber to this game, setting a World Series record with five home runs in the first five innings. They cruised to a big win at home, giving pitcher **Ranger Suárez** great support as he threw five shutout innings. **Bryce Harper** had one of the Phillies' five homers.

GAME 4 Houston 5, Philadelphia 0
The Astros made history by throwing only the

second no-hitter in the 118 years of the World Series. **Cristian Javier** began with six innings, allowing only two walks. **Bryan Abreu**, **Rafael Montero**, and **Ryan Pressly** followed with a no-hit inning apiece. It was the first no-no in the Series since the Yankees' **Don Larsen** threw a perfect game in 1956. The Astros scored all their runs in the fifth inning, in a huge turnaround from being shut out in Game 3.

GAME 5 Houston 3, Philadelphia 2

Veteran ace Verlander led the way on the mound, earning his first World Series win. Rookie **Jeremy Peña** was the hitting star, with a homer and another RBI. Houston shut down the Phillies offense to win this one, but they needed a great ninth-inning catch at the wall by center fielder **Chas McCormick** to ice it.

GAME 6 Houston 4, Philadelphia 1

This game back in Houston was tight until the sixth inning. Philly got its run on a homer by **Kyle Schwarber**, but after that it was all Houston. **Yordan Álvarez** blasted a three-run homer and the Astros bullpen continued its amazing success, shutting down the Phillies' bats. It was the second World Series win by the Astros, who also won in 2017.

The Astros celebrated with the Commissioner's Trophy after their six-game Series win.

2022 MLB Stat Champs

AL Hitting Leaders

62 HOME RUNS
131 RBI
Aaron Judge, Yankees

.316 BATTING AVERAGE
Luis Arráez, Twins

35 STOLEN BASES
Jorge Mateo,
Orioles

*Jeff "Squirrel"
McNeil*

NL Hitting Leaders

46 HOME RUNS
Kyle Schwarber, Phillies

131 RBI
Pete Alonso, Mets

.326 BATTING AVERAGE
Jeff McNeil, Mets

41 STOLEN BASES
Jon Berti, Marlins

AL Pitching Leaders

18 WINS
1.75 ERA
Justin Verlander, Astros

257 STRIKEOUTS
Gerrit Cole, Yankees

42 SAVES
Emmanuel Clase,
Guardians

NL Pitching Leaders

21 WINS
Kyle Wright, Braves

2.16 ERA
Julio Urías, Dodgers

243 STRIKEOUTS
Corbin Burnes,
Brewers

41 SAVES
Kenley Jansen,
Braves

2022 MLB Award Winners

MOST VALUABLE PLAYER

AL: **Aaron Judge**
Yankees

NL: **Paul Goldschmidt**
Cardinals

CY YOUNG AWARD

AL: **Justin Verlander**
Astros

NL: **Sandy Alcántara**
Marlins

ROOKIE OF THE YEAR

AL: **Julio Rodríguez**
Mariners

NL: **Michael Harris II**
Braves

MANAGER OF THE YEAR

AL: **Terry Francona**
Guardians

NL: **Buck Showalter**
Mets

ROBERTO CLEMENTE AWARD

Justin Turner
Dodgers

Aaron Judge

World Baseball Classic

Japan's national team was the champion of the 2023 World Baseball Classic. But everyone agreed: Baseball was the real winner. Huge crowds packed stadiums, while tens of millions watched in countries around the world. The biggest stars faced off and the drama was huge! The only bad part? We have to wait three years for the next one!

GROUP STAGE

Pool A (PLAYED IN TAIWAN)
TOP TWO: **Cuba, Italy**
Every team in this group finished with a 2–2 record! The biggest surprise came when Italy beat Cuba, often a powerful team. After all the tiebreakers were sorted out, both of those teams advanced to the next round.

Italy celebrated a surprise win over Cuba.

Pool B (PLAYED IN JAPAN)
TOP TWO: **Japan, Australia**
Led by megastar **Shohei Ohtani**, Japan dominated this group. They beat China in one game 22-2. The Czech Republic team was made up of part-time players. Czech pitcher **Ondrej Satoria** (who also works as an engineer) struck out Ohtani . . . and Ohtani asked him for a signed jersey!

Pool C (PLAYED IN ARIZONA)
TOP TWO: **Mexico, United States**
A surprise win by the US's southern neighbor made a tough pool tougher. The US needed a big win over Canada (with a nine-run first inning!) to earn a spot in the quarterfinals.

Pool D (PLAYED IN FLORIDA)
TOP TWO: **Venezuela, Puerto Rico**
A shocking win by Colombia over the Dominican Republic meant this group's winners were not set until the final game. A highlight of this pool was a perfect game pitched by four Puerto Rico pitchers in a win over Israel. Puerto Rico then beat the D.R. in the final game to snag the quarterfinals berth.

QUARTERFINALS

Cuba snuck by Australia 4-3. Trea Turner of the US smacked a grand slam to give his team a big 9-7 over Venezuela, which had not lost before that game. Ohtani hit a career-high 102 mph while pitching Japan to a 9-3 win over Italy. Mexico stormed back from being four runs behind to shock Puerto Rico 5-4.

SEMIFINALS

US 14, Cuba 2

American bats continued to be red-hot, with Turner adding two more homers and captain **Mike Trout** banging a two-run double. This was the first game played between US and Cuban national teams since 1959!

Japan 6, Mexico 5

A classic game! Mexico jumped ahead on a three-run homer off Japan's ace, **Roki Sasaki**. But then Japan tied it on a homer by new Red Sox star **Masataka Yoshida**. After Mexico went up by a run in the ninth, Japan roared back with two in the bottom. They won the game on a walk-off two-run double by two-time Nippon Baseball League MVP **Munetaka Murakami**. Wow!

CHAMPIONSHIP GAME

Japan 3, US 2

The best overall player in baseball against the best hitter. Japan vs the United States. Power vs power. With the whole world watching! The title game came down, like a movie script, to Ohtani against Trout. US down by a run, their last hitter at bat. Ohtani blew four 100-mph pitches past Trout. Then mowed him down with a slider. Japan . . . WBA champions for the third time! An instant classic! Both players said it was their career highlight . . . so far!

Angel vs Angel—Ohtani strikes out Trout.

NFL

HERE WE GO AGAIN!

Patrick Mahomes heads for the celebration after leading his team to another Super Bowl win! The superstar Q.B led the Kansas City Chiefs to a thrilling 38-35 win over the Philadelphia Eagles in Super Bowl LVII in February. The all-world passer drove his team to the game-winning field goal and earned his second Super Bowl MVP award as well. Read on to find out how the Chiefs got there . . . plus, check out all the other big 2022 NFL season news!

NFL 2022

The best thing about every new NFL season is that each team starts from scratch. Winning the Super Bowl doesn't guarantee another good season: Players have to earn it all over again. The 2022 season was proof of that. The Los Angeles Rams won Super Bowl LVI over the Cincinnati Bengals. But a few weeks into the 2022 season, both teams looked like they were still tired from that game! The Rams were 2–3, while the Bengals had also lost three games. The Rams never recovered; their 5–12 record was the worst ever for a defending champ. The Bengals did bounce back, winning 10 straight games before losing in the AFC Championship Game. Meanwhile, other teams rose, aiming for their own Super Bowl dreams. The Philadelphia Eagles were the hottest, winning their first seven games and even getting to 13–1 at one point. The Minnesota Vikings were good *and* lucky; nine of their first 10 wins were by a touchdown or less! The Seattle Seahawks lost superstar QB **Russell Wilson** in the offseason. Veteran **Geno Smith** took over and became a surprise star, leading the NFL in completion percentage and throwing a career-high 30 TD passes. The Detroit Lions had their first winning season in five years, led by touchdown machine RB **Jamaal Williams**. San Francisco was down to its third-string QB due to injuries, but its powerful defense led the team to a division title.

Jamaal Williams

Geno Smith

TEAMWORK AND COURAGE

During the Bills–Bengals game in Week 17, Buffalo's **Damar Hamlin** suddenly collapsed. Medical staff from both teams raced to help him. It turned out his heart had stopped. While players from both teams prayed and waited, doctors and trainers aided Hamlin, giving him CPR on the field. The game was canceled while Hamlin was taken to a hospital, where he was able to recover after more treatment. But it was a super-scary moment. Hamlin returned a few weeks later to cheer on his teammates—a credit to fast work by experts and to Hamlin's bravery in recovery.

Meanwhile, in the NFC South, someone had to earn a playoff spot as the champ. But none of the teams could win a lot of games! In fact, Tampa Bay won the division but had a losing record (8–9), only the sixth time that has ever happened.

Other teams that were expected to do well did just that. Kansas City had the best record in the AFC, with the Buffalo Bills right behind.

The 2022 season was also full of records; starting on page 50, check out our week-by-week recap of the best games to find the greatest comeback in NFL history, a new quarterback rushing champ, another mark for the GOAT (also see page 25), the incredible catch of the year, and an unlucky day for a Dallas kicker! Then read on to revisit a very memorable Super Bowl!

2022 Final Regular-Season Standings

AFC EAST	W-L-T	AFC NORTH	W-L-T	AFC SOUTH	W-L-T	AFC WEST	W-L-T
Bills	13–3	Bengals	12–4	Jaguars	9–8	Chiefs	14–3
Dolphins	9–8	Ravens	10–7	Titans	7–10	Chargers	10–7
Patriots	8–9	Steelers	9–8	Colts	4–12–1	Raiders	6–11
Jets	7–10	Browns	7–10	Texans	3–13–1	Broncos	5–12

NFC EAST	W-L-T	NFC NORTH	W-L-T	NFC SOUTH	W-L-T	NFC WEST	W-L-T
Eagles	14–3	Vikings	13–4	Buccaneers	8–9	49ers	13–4
Cowboys	12–5	Lions	9–8	Panthers	7–10	Seahawks	9–8
Giants	9–7–1	Packers	8–9	Saints	7–10	Rams	5–12
Commanders	8–8–1	Bears	3–14	Falcons	7–10	Cardinals	4–13

Weeks 1-4

WEEK 1

Wild Opener:
The last time **Joe Burrow** played, it was in a losing effort in the Super Bowl. Against Pittsburgh in Week 1, Burrow looked anything but super, throwing four interceptions. In a crazy back-and-forth game, Cincinnati had a chance to win in regulation, but Pittsburgh blocked a game-winning extra-point attempt. Then, on the final play of overtime, **Chris Boswell** knocked in a 53-yard field goal. Final score: Steelers 23, Bengals 20!

A New Central King:
Minnesota WR **Justin Jefferson** had a monster game with 184 receiving yards and 2 TDs as the Vikings beat NFC North rival Green Bay 23-7. The Packers' QB **Aaron Rodgers** really missed his own star WR **Davante Adams**, who moved to the Raiders in the offseason. Rodgers threw for only 195 yards.

Baker-less Browns:
Cleveland fans knew what **Baker Mayfield** could do; he was their star QB for four seasons. But he was sent to Carolina in the offseason, so of course those two teams played

Tua Tagovailoa

Week 1. Mayfield was solid, but the Browns' running game led the way. **Nick Chubb** had 141 yards, while **Kareem Hunt** scored 2 TDs. Still, it took a 58-yard field goal with 8 seconds left to make the final score: Browns 26, Panthers 24.

Bad News 'Boys:
Dallas got bad news in the second half of its game against Tampa Bay. Star QB **Dak Prescott** went out with an injured hand. The Cowboys saw more bad news on the scoreboard as they lost to the Bucs 19-3. The news got worse the next day when the team learned Prescott would be out for six to eight weeks after surgery on his throwing hand.

WEEK 2

Comebacks Galore:
Three Week 2 games ended with amazing comebacks. The New York Jets trailed the Cleveland Browns 30-17 with less than two minutes left. Computers gave the Browns a 99.9 percent chance to win. But **Joe Flacco** of the Jets threw 66- and 15-yard TDs to shock the Browns. It was the first time since 2001 a team had rallied from that far behind that late. Also, Miami QB **Tua Tagovailoa** had 4 of his 6 TD passes in the fourth quarter, rallying the Dolphins from

Breece Hall scored late to give the Jets a win.

Fly, Eagles, Fly: Jalen
Hurts became the first player ever with 900 passing yards and 100 rushing yards in his team's first three games. The speedy QB had 3 TD passes, including one to **DeVonta Smith** (who had a career-best 169 receiving yards) on the way to a crushing 24-8 win over Washington. The Commanders' QB was former Eagles star **Carson Wentz**, who was sacked nine times!

WEEK 4

Dak Who?: Well, not really—the Cowboys will welcome back injured QB **Dak Prescott** soon, but backup **Cooper Rush** has become a star. He led Dallas to its third straight win since he took over during Week 1. Rush passed for 2 TDs while steering the Cowboys to a 25-10 win over the division-rival Commanders.

Say Breece to That!: For only the second time ever, the Jets won in Pittsburgh, defeating the Steelers 24-20. RB **Breece Hall** squeezed over the goal line with just 16 seconds left for the winning touchdown. QB **Zach Wilson** got the scoring going for New York with his first NFL TD catch!

Big West Showdown: The Los Angeles Rams were the defending Super Bowl champs. But against their NFC West rivals, the San Francisco 49ers, they sure didn't look like champs! They lost 24-9! The 49ers sacked Rams QB **Matthew Stafford** seven times and scored on an interception return. SF's **Deebo Samuel** had a 57-yard catch-and-run for a score.

21 points down to a 42-38 win over the Ravens. And Arizona was down 20-0 at halftime. But QB **Kyler Murray** worked his magic, tying the score on the game's final play. A 59-yard fumble return in overtime by **Byron Murphy Jr.** gave the Cardinals a 29-23 win over the Raiders.

WEEK 3

KC = L: The Indianapolis Colts pulled off the biggest upset of the young season, beating the high-powered Kansas City Chiefs 20-17. QB **Matt Ryan** led Indy on a game-winning drive that ended with just 24 seconds left and a TD catch by **Jelani Woods**.

Splash!: Miami had an upset of its own, but the way the 3–0 Dolphins were playing, it might turn out not to be a surprise win. It was the Miami defense that led the way in their 21-19 win over the Bills. **Josh Allen** threw 63 passes for the Bills for 400 yards.

Before he led the NFL in rushing in 2022, Josh Jacobs scored 3 TDs against Houston.

Weeks 5–8

WEEK 5

Mr. Clutch: Baltimore K **Justin Tucker** is one of the best ever. His streak of fourth-quarter or later field goals grew to 61 in a row while booting a 43-yard game-winner that made the Ravens 19-17 winners over the Bengals. Earlier in the game, he also made a 58-yard kick!

Jolly Olde Giants: In London, England, the Giants topped the Packers 27-22 when **Saquon Barkley** dove in for a game-winning 2-yard TD. Even though Giants QB **Daniel Jones** had a hurt ankle, he led the team to 17 straight points for the big international win.

Mr. Everything: **Taysom Hill** does it all for the Saints. In their 39-32 win over

Seattle, Hill ran for 3 TDs and also threw a TD pass! He's supposed to be a tight end, but Hill plays RB, QB, WR, and who knows . . . maybe he can even punt!

WEEK 6

AFC Rematch: In the 2021 AFC Championship Game, Kansas City and Buffalo played one of the most memorable games in years. The Chiefs won, but in 2022, the Bills got a little revenge. **Josh Allen** threw a go-ahead TD pass to **Dawson Knox** with just over a minute left and Buffalo won this big AFC showdown 24-20.

Still No Losses: Philadelphia is the last undefeated team left after beating Dallas 26-17. The Eagles' defense intercepted Dallas QB **Cooper Rush** three times, while Philly QB **Jalen Hurts** threw for 2 TDs. "We're going up, up, up, up!" shouted Eagles CB **Darius Slay** after the game.

Minnesota Cook-ing:
The Vikings took control of the NFC North with a 24-16 win over the Dolphins. **Dalvin Cook** ran for a late 53-yard TD to clinch the game and move the Vikings to 5–1.

WEEK 7

Panther Surprise:
The Carolina Panthers had fired their coach, traded their best player, and had a third-string QB starting the game. Oh, and they were facing the GOAT—**Tom Brady** and the Tampa Bay Bucs. But in one of the season's biggest upsets, the Panthers won 21-3. The Carolina defense shut down Brady, while **P.J. Walker** had 2 TD passes in just his fourth career start.

Second-Half Surge:
Raiders RB **Josh Jacobs** scored 3 rushing TDs in the second half to lead Las Vegas to a 38-20 win over the Houston Texans. The Raiders clinched the game on a 73-yard interception-return TD by **Duron Harmon**.

Big Joe:
Bengals QB **Joe Burrow** became the fourth QB ever with 450 or more passing yards (he had 481), 3 TD passes, a rushing TD, and an 80 percent completion rate. He did it all in a big 35-17 win over the Falcons. It was a big win for the defending AFC champs, who moved to 4–3.

WEEK 8

Triple Play:
Christian McCaffrey, in his second game with new team San Francisco, did it all in a big 31-14 win over the Rams. The former Carolina Panthers superstar ran for a score, caught a TD pass, and threw for a TD to **Brandon Aiyuk**. He was the first 49ers runner to do all three in one game, and the eleventh ever.

Mr. 200:
Tennessee's **Derrick Henry** must love playing Houston. In four games against the Texans, he has run for 150 or more yards and 2 TDs, including in this Titans' 17-10 win over the Texans. Henry's 219 yards also put him into a tie for most 200-yard games ever, with six.

New No. 2:
With New England's 22-17 win over the Jets, coach **Bill Belichick** moved into second place all-time in coaching wins. It was the 325th W of his career; that total includes 31 wins in the postseason, including six Super Bowl titles, also a record. He passed Chicago legend **George Halas** and now trails only Miami coach **Don Shula**, who had 347 wins.

Belichick: He's No. 2!

Weeks 9-12

WEEK 9

★ Mix for Six Times Five: Bengals RB **Joe Mixon** set a team record with 5 TDs (4 rushing and 1 receiving) to lead Cincinnati to a 42-21 win over Carolina. Mixon also ran for 153 yards to make Cincy and fantasy football fans very happy!

★ Rushing Record: Chicago's **Justin Fields** set a new all-time single-game rushing record for QBs by sprinting for 178 yards. He also threw 3 TDs, but his success was not enough to overcome Miami and 3 TDs from **Tua Tagovailoa**. The Dolphins won an offense-heavy game 35-32.

Record-setter Justin Fields

WEEK 10

★ Game of the Year?: All the Bills had to do to beat the one-loss Vikings was snap the ball. But Buffalo QB **Josh Allen** couldn't make the play, which started right near the goal line. The fumble was recovered by Minnesota in the end zone, giving the Vikes the lead with just 41 seconds left. Incredibly, Allen then led the Bills to a game-tying **Tyler Bass** field goal with two seconds left! In overtime, the Vikings worked a long drive to a field goal by **Greg Joseph**. **Patrick Peterson** then made his second interception to seal the 33-30 win for the Vikings. Bonus: In the game, **Justin Jefferson** of the Vikings made what may have been the best one-handed, steal-the-ball-from-the-defender catch ever! You've got to see it to believe it!

★ International Football: **Tom Brady** of the Bucs became the first player to win an NFL game in four countries. He led Tampa Bay to a big 21-16 win over Seattle in Germany. It was the first NFL game ever in that country, and the victory gave Brady yet another record. His win in Germany joined previous victories in Mexico, England, and of course, the US in his GOAT career. Oh, and Tampa Bay moved into first place!

★ Tua Terrific: Miami QB Tua Tagovailoa had 3 TD passes for the third straight game—that made a total of 9 TD throws with no interceptions. His latest great game led Dolphins fans to chant, "MVP! MVP!" Miami beat Cleveland 39-17.

Jefferson's catch is better on video!

✱ Rookie Coach: Jeff Saturday had never coached in high school or college, but he did win a Super Bowl during his 14 year NFL career. Still, he was an odd choice as the Colts' new coach. But he got a win in his first game in charge, as Indianapolis beat the struggling Las Vegas Raiders 25-20.

✱ Eagles Grounded: The Washington Commanders defense forced 4 turnovers to upset the undefeated Eagles 32-21. Washington's rushing game played a big part, too, piling up 152 yards and a pair of TDs.

✱ He's Still Got It: QB Aaron Rodgers and the Packers were struggling. They had lost five in a row heading into a big game against Dallas. Rookie WR

Christian Watson came up big with 3 TD catches. Rodgers led the Pack on a drive in overtime that ended with Mason Crosby's game-winning field goal.

WEEK 11

✱ Lions Roar!: Detroit has had some tough seasons lately, but 2022 was looking good when the Lions won their third straight game, 31-18 over the Giants in an upset. RB Jamaal Williams led the way with 3 TDs. A surprisingly tough Lions D held Giants star Saquon Barkley to just 22 yards rushing.

✱ Mr. Comeback: Down by four with just 1:46 left, Patrick Mahomes was magic again. The Chiefs QB led his team on a quick-strike drive that ended with Travis Kelce's third TD of the day. That gave the Chiefs a 30-27 win over the Chargers and another entry for Mahomes' list of comebacks.

WEEK 12

✱ Raider Rumble: The Raiders beat Seattle 40-34 in overtime, but the big story was Vegas RB Josh Jacobs. He set a Raiders team record with 229 rushing yards, including an 86-yard sprint for the game-ending score. Jacobs also had 74 yards receiving; he was only the fourth player since 1950 to score twice while piling up 300 yards from scrimmage.

✱ Jalen Hurts Packers: Philly QB Jalen Hurts continued his amazing season, setting a team QB rushing record with 157 yards as he led his team to a 40-33 win over the Packers. Hurts also became the first QB in NFL history to have at least 150 passing yards, 150 rushing yards, and 2 passing TDs in the same game.

Weeks 13-16

WEEK 13

★ **Tough Break:** The 49ers won *and* lost this week. They won by beating Miami 33-17 to stay atop the NFC West. They lost because starting QB **Jimmy Garoppolo** suffered a broken foot, ending his season. He was already replacing original starter **Trey Lance**, so the Niners would be down to QB No. 3 for the rest of 2022.

★ **Dallas Domination:** Talk about finishing strong. Dallas piled up 33 points in the fourth quarter—the third-most in NFL history—to sprint away from Indianapolis for a 54-19 win. The Cowboys had four takeaways in the final quarter, including a fumble-return TD by **Malik Hooker**.

★ **Brady Does It Again:** For the NFL-record-setting 44th time in his career, **Tom Brady** led his team to victory after it trailed in the fourth quarter. His pass to **Rachaad White** with just three seconds left was the latest of those wins, as the Bucs came back to beat the Saints 17-16.

WEEK 14

★ **Magic Mayfield:** On Tuesday morning of Week 14, **Baker Mayfield** didn't have a job. On Thursday night, he was a game-winning hero. What happened? Mayfield was let go by the Panthers, but on Dec. 6 signed with the Rams as a backup. Two days later in LA's Thursday night game against the Raiders, Mayfield was brought on . . . and he led the team to a shocking come-from-behind 17-16 win. He threw the game-winning TD to **Van Jefferson** with nine seconds left!

★ **Purdy Good:** On paper, the 49ers vs. the Bucs was a battle of QBs drafted very late by NFL teams—one in the sixth round and the other as the last player of the seventh round. However, the former sixth-rounder was Brady, the GOAT; the seventh-rounder was rookie **Brock Purdy**. Surprise! Purdy and the Niners upset Brady and the Bucs 35-7, as Purdy threw 2 TDs and ran for another.

Mayfield came in the nick of time!

WEEK 15

✴ Very Bad Pass:

The Patriots lost to the Raiders on what might have been the dumbest play in NFL history. Tied 24-24, the Patriots ran one last play from their own 45-yard line as time ran out. Instead of falling down and moving to overtime, Pats players started tossing laterals. **Jakobi Meyers** threw the last one, but it went to the Raiders' **Chandler Jones**. He bowled over Pats QB **Mac Jones** and ran 48 yards for a game-winning TD. Raiders 30-24, wow!

Minnesota's Dalvin Cook

✴ Top Comeback Ever:

The Vikings were down 33-0 to the Colts at halftime. Minnesota defensive back **Patrick Peterson** told the offense at halftime, "You just need [to score] 5 touchdowns." Well . . . Minnesota did! They completed the biggest comeback in a game in NFL history by scoring 36 second-half points to tie the game. They won the game 39-36 in the final seconds of overtime on a field goal by **Greg Joseph**.

✴ Streak Breaker:

The AFC's Jacksonville Jaguars were having a tough season, with several close losses. They entered their game against Dallas having lost 20 straight games to NFC teams. That streak ended in overtime when **Rayshawn Jenkins** snatched a tipped pass out of the air and returned the pick 52 yards for a game-ending TD, 40-34.

WEEK 16

✴ Remember Franco:

Four days before the Steelers were going to retire his jersey, the great running back **Franco Harris** passed away suddenly. He was 72. But the team had the ceremony anyway. Fans were then thrilled when the team pulled off a big comeback to beat the Raiders 13-10 on a late TD pass from **Kenny Pickett** to **George Pickens**.

✴ Charging to the Playoffs:

San Diego clinched a postseason spot when its defense shut down the Colts 20-3. **Austin Ekeler** led the way on offense, running for 2 TDs while catching 4 passes to reach a team-best 101 for the season.

✴ Panthers Prowl:

Carolina set a team record with 320 rushing yards in a 37-23 win over the Lions. **D'Onta Foreman** had 165 of them, along with a TD. **Chuba Hubbard** chipped in 125 yards more. The game was played in a wind chill of 9. Yes . . . 9. (Of course, it was a wind-chill temperature of −12 in Chicago when the Bills beat the Bears 35-13!)

✴ Miracle Vikes:

Minnesota K Greg Joseph smacked a 61-yard field goal on the final play to give his team a 27-24 win over the Giants. It was the Vikings' NFL-record 11th win of one score or less and the third walk-off game-winner for Joseph in 2022.

Weeks 17-18

Allen and the Jags ran to the playoffs!

✱ Nine for Niners: RB **Christian McCaffrey** led the way with 121 yards rushing (and a TD) and 72 yards receiving as San Francisco won its ninth game in a row. It took overtime, though, after the Raiders tied the game. **Robbie Gould** kicked a short field goal for a 37-34 win.

✱ Bucs Are Back!: **Tom Brady** won his NFL-record 19th division title when he led the Buccaneers to a 30-24 win over the Panthers. Brady had 3 TD passes to **Mike Evans** among his 432 passing yards. Evans also became the first player ever with 1,000 yards receiving in each of his first nine seasons.

WEEK 18

✱ Scooping Up a Spot: The winners between Jacksonville and Tennessee would earn a playoff spot. The Jaguars were trailing, but a scoop-and-score fumble return TD by LB **Josh Allen** gave them a 20-16 win. It is the Jags' first playoff since 2017.

✱ Lions Spoil Pack: The Seahawks were the biggest Detroit Lions fans around on the season's final Sunday. If the Lions beat Green Bay, Seattle would earn a playoff spot—and Detroit did! The Lions won 20-16 to send Seattle onward.

✱ Miami Magic: Also on that final Sunday, the Dolphins needed to beat the Jets and hope the Patriots lost to Buffalo. The Bills did their part, knocking off New England 35-23. The Dolphins did theirs, beating the Jets 11-6. Hello, playoffs!

WEEK 17

✱ Giant Win for Giants: For the first time in six seasons, the Giants will be in the playoffs. A 38-10 win over the Colts clinched their spot. QB **Daniel Jones** led the way as he had all year, throwing 2 TD passes and running for 2 more scores.

✱ Pats Power: New England surprised Miami with a 23-21 win and kept its playoff hopes alive. A late pick-six by the Pats, **Kyle Dugger**, gave New England the lead on the way to its first win over Miami in the last five meetings.

Wild-Card Playoffs

49ers 41, Seahawks 23

Seattle held a surprising halftime lead, but the Niners rallied with 25 points in the second half. Rookie surprise **Brock Purdy** threw 3 TD passes and ran for another. Purdy was the first rookie in 85 years with at least 200 passing yards and 2 TDs in a playoff game. The big play for the Niners came from **Deebo Samuel**, who took a short pass and galloped 74 yards for a key late score.

Giants 31, Vikings 24

Daniel Jones passed for 2 TDs and **Saquon Barkley** ran for 2 TDs to end Minnesota's surprising season. It was the first playoff win in 11 seasons for the Giants.

Cowboys 31, Buccaneers 14

Dak Prescott led the way with 3 TD passes and a TD run. TE **Dalton Schultz** caught 2 of those TDs. Even **Tom Brady**'s career-high 66 pass attempts were not enough to beat Big D. Dallas K **Brett Maher** set an unfortunate all-time NFL record, missing 4 extra-point attempts.

Jaguars 31, Chargers 30

In the third-biggest comeback in NFL history, Jacksonville rallied from 27-0 to win on a last-play field goal. Jags QB **Trevor Lawrence** overcame 4 first-half interceptions by throwing 4 second-half TDs, while the Jags defense held the Chargers to just a field goal in the second half.

Bills 34, Dolphins 31

Miami gave Buffalo all it could handle, turning an expected blowout into a tight game. Miami, playing with its third-string QB, led 24-20 early in the third quarter, but then Buffalo QB **Josh Allen** threw two quick TDs to retake the lead for good.

Bengals 24, Ravens 17

As Baltimore tried for a go-ahead TD, the Bengals' **Sam Hubbard** recovered a fumble and returned it 98 yards for a game-winning score. The surprisingly tough win kept Bengals' hopes for a Super Bowl return alive.

Brock Purdy

Cincinnati's Joe Burrow had to pass through snowflakes for a playoff win.

Divisional Playoffs

Eagles 38, Giants 7

Hurts wasn't hurt anymore! The Eagles superstar QB, **Jalen Hurts**, showed that he was fully back from late-season injuries. He threw 2 TD passes and ran for another score as Philly crushed their NFC East rivals. The Eagles ran for 268 yards, while holding the Giants to only 118.

Chiefs 27, Jaguars 20

When KC QB **Patrick Mahomes** left the game with an injured ankle, Jacksonville fans might have thought, "This is our chance!" Not so fast! Though limping, Mahomes came back in the second half to lead his team to its fifth straight AFC Championship Game.

49ers 19, Cowboys 12

Turnovers played a big part in this defensive battle. Dallas QB **Dak Prescott**'s 2 interceptions contributed to his team's low score. Niners K **Robbie Gould** nailed 4 field goals. A third-stringer when the season started, SF QB **Brock Purdy** had taken his team one step from the Super Bowl.

Bengals 27, Bills 10

QB **Joe Burrow** led his team to its eighth win in a row. Cincy led 14-0 after the first quarter, thanks to Burrow's TDs to **Ja'Marr Chase** and **Hayden Hurst**. Then the Bengals D never let the Bills back in the game on that snowy day in Buffalo.

Conference Championships

Hurts helped the Eagles fly to the Super Bowl.

NFC

Eagles 31, 49ers 7

The Cinderella story of Niners QB **Brock Purdy** ended on the first drive, when he was hurt while being sacked. San Francisco's fourth QB of the season, **Josh Johnson**, had to come in. The Eagles took full advantage, not letting the Niners score after the first quarter. Meanwhile, **Jalen Hurts** led a powerful rushing attack that included 4 TDs on the ground. The Eagles fly back to the Super Bowl for the first time since the 2017 season.

AFC

Chiefs 23, Bengals 20

Kansas City won this rematch of the previous AFC title game thanks to a gritty **Patrick Mahomes**. He had hurt his ankle in a win over the Jaguars, so he could barely run! But he could throw, and he tossed a pair of TDs and had 326 passing yards. He drove his team to the game-winning field goal, a 45-yarder by **Harrison Butker**, with three seconds left! The Bengals played well, but penalties and interceptions hurt their cause. The Chiefs head to their third Super Bowl in five seasons.

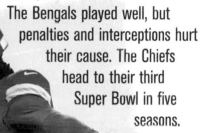

Harrison Butker

Super Bowl LVII
KANSAS CITY 38, PHILADELPHIA 35

Hurts muscled his way in for a key late touchdown.

How did we get there? The Eagles scored on the game's opening drive. QB **Jalen Hurts** scored the first of his 3 rushing TDs—the first QB and second player ever to do that in a Super Bowl. Mahomes connected with star TE **Travis Kelce** for a TD to match the Eagles. Hurts then hit **A.J. Brown** with a long TD pass. The next time the Eagles had the ball, though, Hurts fumbled. The ball was picked up by KC's **Nick Bolton**, who ran 36 yards on a scoop-and-score to tie the game at 14-14.

However, the Eagles bounced back with 10 more points on another Hurts run and a field goal by **Jake Elliott** to make their halftime lead 24-14.

Something magic must have happened in the Chiefs locker room. Coaches on both sides of the ball made changes, Mahomes had time to rest his ankle, and Kelce made a powerful speech to his teammates. It all came together in a dominating second half.

The Chiefs scored touchdowns on each of their first three drives, while the Eagles managed only a field goal. The third KC TD, for a 35-27 lead, was set up by a 65-yard punt

What happened at halftime? When the Eagles headed to the locker room (while Rihanna performed on the field!), they were ahead 24-14. They had run twice as many plays and gained twice as many yards as the Chiefs. KC QB **Patrick Mahomes** seemed to have reinjured his ankle late in the first half. Philly fans were feeling good!

But in the second half, the Chiefs took over. It was one of the best halves of football ever in a Super Bowl game. Kansas City scored every time it had the ball, did not commit a penalty or a turnover, and capped the game with a 27-yard field goal with eight seconds left for the winning points. What a turnaround!

return by **Kadarius Toney** of the Chiefs, the longest in Super Bowl history!

Hurts was not done, though. He drove the Eagles to a touchdown, and then pounded over for a two-point conversion: tie game, 35-35!

Mahomes took over with about five minutes left and Philly never got another good chance. The Super Bowl MVP led a 13-play drive to the Philly 1-yard line. The drive included his 26-yard run on his bad ankle for a big first down. A late penalty on the Eagles helped the Chiefs run the clock down before **Harrison Butker**'s game-winning kick.

It was the Chiefs' second Super Bowl win in four seasons, and Mahomes became the first player ever with two Super Bowl wins and MVP awards in his first six seasons.

SUPER BROTHERS!

KC's **Travis Kelce** and Philly's **Jason Kelce** became the first brothers to play each other in a Super Bowl. Their mom wore a shirt that was half Chiefs and half Eagles!

This Super Bowl record punt return by Kadarius Toney set up a huge Chiefs TD.

NFL Awards 2022

MOST VALUABLE PLAYER
PATRICK MAHOMES
CHIEFS

OFFENSIVE PLAYER OF THE YEAR
JUSTIN JEFFERSON
VIKINGS

DEFENSIVE PLAYER OF THE YEAR
NICK BOSA
49ERS

OFFENSIVE ROOKIE OF THE YEAR
GARRETT WILSON
JETS

DEFENSIVE ROOKIE OF THE YEAR
SAUCE GARDNER
JETS

COACH OF THE YEAR
BRIAN DABOLL
GIANTS

WALTER PAYTON
NFL MAN OF THE YEAR
DAK PRESCOTT
COWBOYS

Patrick
Mahomes

2022 Stats Champs

5,250 PASSING YARDS
41 PASSING TDS
Patrick Mahomes, Chiefs

1,653 RUSHING YARDS
Josh Jacobs, Raiders

17 RUSHING TDS
Jamaal Williams, Lions

128 RECEPTIONS
1,809 RECEIVING YARDS
Justin Jefferson, Vikings

14 RECEIVING TDS
Davante Adams, Raiders

184 TACKLES
Foyesade Oluokun, Jaguars

37 FIELD GOALS
Justin Tucker, Ravens

18.5 SACKS
Nick Bosa, 49ers

143 POINTS
Jason Myers, Seahawks

Davante
Adams

FANTASY STARS 2022

Some familiar names moved to the top of the scoring charts in 2022, but wise fantasy owners also were able to predict the rise of some young stars! How did your team do?

POSITION/PLAYER/POINTS

QB	**Patrick Mahomes**	417.40
RB	**Austin Ekeler**	372.70
WR	**Justin Jefferson**	368.66
TE	**Travis Kelce**	316.30
K	**Justin Tucker**	158.00
DST	**Patriots**	173.00

Source: NFL.com Fantasy

XFL 2023

The NFL was not the only football game in town. The XFL first played through 2001, but then shut down. In 2023, acting superstar and former pro wrestler **Dwayne "The Rock" Johnson** was one of the league's new owners, and he brought it back with razzle-dazzle action. The first season ended with a surprising champion. The Arlington Renegades were just 4–6 on the season, but put together a magical playoff run. They had lost to Houston in the season's final game, but then beat them in the semifinals! In the final, QB **Luis Perez**, who had joined the team late in the season, had 3 TD passes and 288 passing yards. Arlington was the big underdog again, but beat the D.C. Defenders 35-26.

Luis Perez

2023 HALL OF FAME CLASS

◄◄◄ CB/S Ronde Barber
16 seasons with Tampa Bay, NFL all-time leader in sacks by CB, All-Decade Team of the 2000s

LB Chuck Howley
Hard-hitting six-time Pro Bowl player, MVP of Super Bowl V (only award winner to come from the losing team)

DT Joe Klecko
Earned Pro Bowl spots at three positions on defensive line, 1981 defensive player of the year, 11 seasons with Jets

CB Darrelle Revis
Best "cover" corner of 2010s, seven-time Pro Bowler, helped Patriots win Super Bowl XLIX

CB Ken Riley
Fifth all-time with 65 career interceptions, three-time AFC interceptions leader, 15 seasons with Bengals

OT Joe Thomas ►►►
10-time Pro Bowler, top OL of the All Decade Team of the 2010s, played record 10,363 snaps in a row, allowed only 30 career sacks

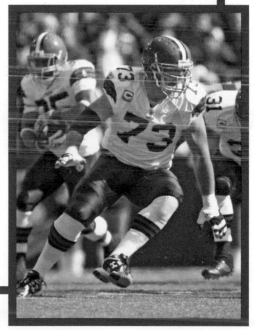

LB Zach Thomas
Five-time first-team All-Pro, 1996 defensive rookie of the year, seven-time Pro Bowler

LB/DE DeMarcus Ware
Two-time NFL sacks leader, four-time first-team All-Pro, nine-time Pro Bowler

Coach Don Coryell
Pioneer in passing offense, led Cardinals and Chargers to division titles, coach of the year awards in 1974 and 1979

COLLEGE FOOTBALL

GOING FOR TWO!

Georgia's defense, led by Christopher Smith (29) and Javon Bullard (22) were a big part of the Bulldogs' dominating 65-7 National Championship victory over TCU. Bullard had 2 interceptions and recovered a fumble. Georgia also had 5 sacks as they won back-to-back national titles!

College Football 2022

The surprises in the 2022 College Football Playoff were about what teams were NOT. Alabama was NOT there; it missed the "final four" for only the second time. TCU was NOT ranked before the season but made it to the title game. The conference with two playoff teams was NOT the SEC . . . it was the Big Ten! In the end, fans saw what had NOT happened since 2012— a repeat champion, the Georgia Bulldogs. You can read about the exciting Playoff games (and the not-so-exciting championship battle) starting on page 80.

Before the Playoff, though, the biggest news in college football in 2022 won't actually happen until 2024. That's the year that will see the College Football Playoff expand to 12 teams! Plus, that season USC and UCLA will lead six other schools leaving the Pac-12 to other conferences. Without those schools, the Pac-12 will fall out of the national picture—the Big Five conferences will become the Big Four.

In the meantime, the 2022 season was packed with incredible games, plays, and players. More than in most recent seasons, the 2022 campaign saw a lot of new teams enter the (four-team, for now) Playoff picture. While Alabama suffered early losses, Tennessee was among the country's best teams. The Volunteers' win over the Crimson Tide (page 75) was one of the wildest and biggest games of the season. Georgia claimed the No. 1 spot for the first time in '22 by beating Tennessee soon after, on a Saturday that saw three of the top six teams lose. TCU put on a great show, earning its first-ever Playoff spot, although it almost missed after a late-season loss. In the west, Utah fell just short of its own first-time Playoff (even though it won

Caleb Williams, USC

Jabari Small (2) helped Tennessee win.

the Pac-12 title with a win that knocked USC out of the Playoff!).

USC did have a highlight in 2022 with the incredible play of Heisman Trophy winner **Caleb Williams** of USC. He combined passing excellence (42 TDs) with running skills (10 TDs on the ground) and brought the Trojans back into the national picture.

A pair of Big Ten teams battled their conference foes and each other but ended up together in the Playoff. Michigan and Ohio State's annual rivalry heated up more than usual when their regular-season matchup turned into one of the best and most important games of the season. The Wolverines ended up the big winners, but the Buckeyes got a Playoff spot anyway!

While few bowl games offered any highlights, the Cotton Bowl is worth remembering. Tulane trailed USC by 15 points with less than five minutes left. Then a touchdown, a safety, and another TD gave them a shocking win. In the past five college seasons, teams in Tulane's position had one victory and lost 1,692 times! Credit the Green Wave with never giving up and winning 46-45.

Read on for more exciting stories from another college football season you will NOT want to forget!

Mark Gronowski, South Dakota State

BEYOND THE PLAYOFF

Here's a salute to the champions of other college football divisions:

FCS: South Dakota State

DIVISION II: Ferris State

DIVISION III: North Central (IL)

NAIA: Northwestern (IA)

September

→ There's an "App" for That: North Carolina held on to beat Appalachian State 63-61 in a game that included 62 total points in the fourth quarter alone (40 by Appalachian State, but it wasn't enough)! Three TDs were scored in the game's final 31 seconds and only a missed two-point try decided the winner. App State did better a week later with a HUGE 17-14 upset of No. 6 Texas A&M.

→ Domers Down: After being ranked fifth and losing to No. 2 Ohio State in their first game, the Notre Dame Fighting Irish expected to bounce back against unranked Marshall. Not so fast! The Thundering Herd (you have to love that awesome nickname!) shocked the Irish at home with a 26-21 upset. Marshall RB **Khalan Laborn** ran for 163 yards and a touchdown to lead the Herd to a surprise win.

Notre Dame had no answers for Marshall's Khalan Laborn in an early-season upset.

→ **Oops:** Late in the Pitt–West Virginia game, a ball bounced off a WVU player's hands and right to Pitt's **Marlin Devonshire**. He sprinted 56 yards for the game-clinching pick-six in a 35-31 Pitt win.

→ **Bama Says "Whew!":** In front of more than 100,000 burnt-orange–wearing Texas fans, No. 1 Alabama nearly lost its first early-season game in years. The Longhorns' defense was outstanding, shutting down 2021 Heisman winner **Bryce Young** and the Bama offense. Texas took a lead on a long field goal but left Young too much time. He drove the Crimson Tide to a 33-yard field goal with ten seconds left to win 20-19.

→ **Tired Players:** Eastern Kentucky and Bowling Green were having so much fun playing each other, they just kept going . . . and going . . . and going. It took *seven* overtimes before EKU won 59-57 on a final two-point conversion.

→ **A Pair of Pac-12 Ws:** The Pac-12 was shocked to hear that USC and UCLA were leaving in the 2024 season. But the Washington Huskies showed that the conference is not through yet. They upset No. 11 Michigan State 39-28. QB **Michael Penix Jr.** threw for 397 yards and 4 TDs. Meanwhile, No. 25 Oregon bounced back from earlier losses to upset No. 12 BYU 41-20.

→ **Almost an Upset:** Wake Forest almost upset No. 5 Clemson, but lost in double OT 51-45. Clemson's **DJ Uiagalelei** threw 5 TD passes, the last in OT to **Davis Allen**. Defensive back **Nate Wiggins** made a game-saving block of Wake Forest's final pass to clinch the win.

Clemson's do-it-all QB, DJ Uiagalelei

→ **Roll On, You Bears:** California broke a six-game losing streak to Arizona, thanks to 274 rushing yards from **Jaydn Ott**. He had TD runs of 73 and 72 yards to help the Golden Bears win 49-31.

→ **Victory Vols:** Tennessee broke a six-game losing streak of its own, beating Florida for only the second time in 18 tries as well. The Volunteers QB **Hendon Hooker** had 2 TD passes and a TD run, and No. 11 Tennessee beat No. 20 Florida 38-33.

October

→ **Wildcats Whimper:** On a Saturday that saw 10 of the Top 25 teams lose, the highest-ranked team to fall was the No. 7 Kentucky Wildcats. Mississippi forced turnovers on each of Kentucky's final two possessions, both times recovering fumbles in the red zone, to prevent a comeback and hold for a 22-19 win.

→ **Switch at the Top:** No. 1 Georgia barely held on to beat unranked Missouri, while Alabama smashed No. 20 Arkansas 49-26. After the weekend, Bama moved into first place in the rankings, even though Georgia got more first-place votes!

→ **Oh No, Oklahoma!:** The No. 18 Oklahoma Sooners were crushed by Big 12 rival TCU 55-24. The Horned Frogs piled up an impressive 668 yards of offense, including 4 TD plays that went 60 yards or more! It was TCU's first win in the last nine meetings between the two schools.

→ **NFL Connection:** Marvin **Harrison** was a star receiver in the NFL for 13 seasons. His son, **Marvin Jr.**, is following in Dad's cleat-steps at No. 3 Ohio State. Junior caught 3 of QB **C.J. Stroud**'s school record-tying 6 TD passes as the Buckeyes stomped Michigan State 49-20.

→ **Record Run:** Israel **Abanikanda** piled up a school-record 320 yards rushing—and scored 6 TDs!—to almost single-handedly lead Pittsburgh to a 45-29 win over Virginia Tech.

Record-setting runner Abanikanda

→ **Here Come the Horned Frogs:** No. 17 TCU and its awesome mascot continued an unbeaten season by defeating No. 19 Kansas. TCU capped a comeback on a TD pass from **Max Duggan** to **Quentin Johnson** with less than two minutes left to win 38-31. The following week, TCU shocked No. 8 Oklahoma State to win 43-40 in double overtime!

→ **Pac-12 Power?:** No. 18 UCLA had one of its biggest wins in recent seasons, moving to 6–0 on the season by knocking off No. 11 Utah 42-32. Bruins QB **Dorian Thompson-Robinson** ran for a score and threw for four more to lead the way.

→ **To the River!:** Tennessee pulled off the biggest win of the young season, defeating No. 3 Alabama 52-49 in a wild game. The Volunteers had lost 15 games in a row to the Crimson Tide, but got 5 TD receptions from **Jalin Hyatt** and a final-play field goal from **Chase McGrath** for a huge win. After McGrath's kick sailed through, Tennessee fans stormed the field. They tore down a goalpost and carried it out of the stadium, where they threw it into the Tennessee River!

→ **Big Ten Battle:** No. 5 Michigan held on to the top spot in the Big Ten with a win over No. 10 Penn State. The Wolverines had two 60-plus-yard TD runs in the 41-17 win. Penn State had been allowing only about 80 rushing yards per game, but Michigan piled up 418 yards on the ground!

→ **Cowboys Stumble:** No. 9 Oklahoma State was on a roll, looking like one of the top teams in the country, until it played No. 22 Kansas State. KSU shocked the Cowboys, shutting them out 48-0. **Will Howard** had 4 TD passes for KSU, while it was the first shutout loss by OSU since 2009.

→ **J.T.'s Big Day:** No. 2 Ohio State defensive end **J.T. Tuimoloau** put the Buckeyes on his back and carried them to a big 44-31 win over Big Ten rival Penn State. J.T. had a fourth-quarter strip sack and

recovered the fumble, then later returned an interception for a touchdown. It was his second pick of the day to go with 2 sacks and 6 tackles. **TreVeyon Henderson**'s 2 rushing scores led the way for the Buckeyes' offense.

Ohio State's Marvin Harrison Jr.

Michigan's Donovan Edwards sealed his team's big win with 2 long TD runs.

November

→ **Bulldogs Bounce Back:** Georgia was pushed down to No. 3 in the first official College Football Playoff rankings. They must not have liked the move, because they swamped No. 1 Tennessee 27-13 to recapture the top spot. **Stetson Bennett** threw 2 TDs for the Bulldogs and ran for another score. The win put Georgia on track for the SEC title game and a shot at the College Football Playoff.

→ **Irish Eyes Were Smiling:** In one of the season's biggest surprise wins, Notre Dame knocked off No. 4 Clemson 35-14. It was Clemson's first loss in 14 games. The Fighting Irish scored on a blocked punt and a 96-yard interception return. Two ND runners, **Logan Diggs** and **Audric Estimé**, each went over 100 yards.

→ **The Tide Turns:** Alabama was one of three top-six teams to lose on the first Saturday in November as they were stunned by No. 10 LSU. The back-and-forth game thrilled LSU home fans, and Alabama needed a game-tying field goal to force overtime. Then **Jayden Daniels** of LSU scored a TD. Instead of kicking the extra point, LSU went for the win and made the two-point conversion to upset the Crimson Tide 32-31.

→ Down Go the Ducks:

No. 6 Oregon, the Pac-12 team with the best shot at the Playoff, was upset by Washington 37-34. The Ducks gambled late in the game and lost. With the score tied at 34-34, Oregon went for it on fourth down inside the Huskies' territory. The play failed and Washington kicked what proved to be the winning field goal soon after.

→ Escape Artists:

A pair of top-four teams barely escaped on November 19. No. 3 Michigan squeaked past Illinois 19-17. The Wolverines needed a field goal by **Jake Moody**, with just nine seconds left for the final points. No. 4 TCU made it even closer. The Horned Frogs trailed Baylor late in the game. TCU also had no timeouts. But their field-goal unit hustled on, just in time for **Griffin Kell**'s last-play field goal, giving TCU a 29-28 win.

→ Pac-12 Battle:

USC and UCLA played their annual rivalry game, and it was a thriller. Both teams scored a pair of TDs in the final quarter, but UCLA fell short, running out of time in a 48-45 loss. USC QB **Caleb Williams** was a star, passing for 470 yards with 2 passing and 1 rushing TD. UCLA's **Dorian Thompson-Robinson** had even better numbers, with 4 TD passes and 2 TD runs. But his late interception sealed the win for the Trojans.

→ "The Game":

That's what No. 2 Ohio State and No. 3 Michigan call their big rivalry. The 2022 version was one of the biggest ever. It was the first time in 16 years both were undefeated before their matchup. Michigan QB **J.J. McCarthy** threw 2 long TD passes in the first half, and then the Wolverines added 4 TDs in the second half to win 45-23. **Donovan Edwards** had TD runs of 75 and 85 yards!

→ A&M and W:

Texas A&M shocked No. 5 LSU 38-23 to knock the Tigers out of a chance at the College Football Playoff. RB **Devon Achane** led the way for the Aggies with 215 rushing yards and a pair of TDs, and A&M also returned a fumble for a score.

→ Orange Out:

No. 8 Clemson and its orange-clad fans still hoped for a Playoff spot. South Carolina ended that dream with a 31-30 win. South Carolina fell behind early but rallied to knock off its in-state rival.

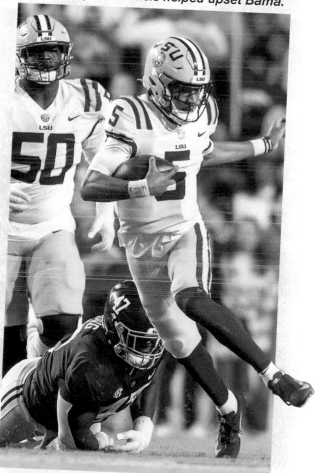

LSU QB Jayden Daniels helped upset Bama.

2022 Conference Championships

PAC-12 Utah 47, USC 24

The No. 4 Trojans lost their chance at the College Football Playoff with their second loss to the Utes in 2022. Star QB **Caleb Williams** was slowed by a leg injury. That let Utah's pass rush catch up to him, and he was sacked 7 times. Meanwhile, Utah QB **Cameron Rising** was excellent, throwing 3 TDs and leading several long drives.

BIG 12 Kansas State 31, TCU 28

Another Playoff team lost, but managed to hold on to its spot in the final four. In an overtime thriller, KSU stopped the Horned Frogs on two plays at the goal line. That opened the door for **Ty Zentner** to bang home a game-winning field goal.

BIG TEN Michigan 43, Purdue 22

The No. 2 Wolverines took care of business, stomping the Boilermakers for a second straight conference title. Michigan won 13 games for the first time in its long football history. **Donovan Edwards** ran for 185 yards and 1 TD, and **J.J. McCarthy** passed for 3 TDs.

AAC Tulane 45, Central Florida 28

The last time Tulane played in a major bowl was in 1939 . . . before World War II! With this big win, they earned a spot in the Cotton Bowl with an 11–2 record. That's a big jump from 2021's 2–10. QB **Michael Pratt** did most of the damage, throwing for 394 yards and 4 TDs. Star RB

Pratt led Tulane to a historic win.

Tyjae Spears added 199 yards rushing before fans stormed the field.

ACC Clemson 39, N. Carolina 10

Defense led the way for the Tigers to be ACC champions for the seventh time in the past eight seasons. CB **Nate Wiggins** was the star, breaking up two goal-line passes and blocking a field goal, along with returning a pick 98 yards for a score.

College Football Awards

HEISMAN TROPHY
WALTER CAMP AWARD
MAXWELL AWARD
QB **Caleb Williams**
USC

BEDNARIK AWARD (DEFENSE)
NAGURSKI TROPHY (DEFENSE)
LB **Will Anderson Jr.**
Alabama

OUTLAND TROPHY (LINEMAN)
C **Olusegun Oluwatimi**
Michigan

BILETNIKOFF AWARD (WIDE RECEIVER)
WR **Jalin Hyatt**
Tennessee

DOAK WALKER AWARD (RUNNING BACK)
RB **Bijan Robinson**
Texas

JIM THORPE AWARD (DEFENSIVE BACK)
CB **Tre'Vius Hodges-Tomlinson**
TCU

LOU GROZA AWARD (KICKER)
K **Christopher Dunn**
NC State

Bijan Robinson, Texas

College Football Semifinals

TCU 51, Michigan 45

In 2021, TCU won only five games. They started the 2022 season unranked. But with a powerful offensive performance in this game, they got a shot at a national championship. The amazing turnaround was helped by 2 interception return TDs by the Horned Frogs and 4 TDs (2 pass, 2 run) from QB **Max Duggan**. The 96 total points were the second-most ever in a Playoff game.

Georgia 42, Ohio State 41

Defending champ Georgia scored 18 points in the fourth quarter to rally for the win in another wild Playoff game. **Stetson Bennett**'s third TD pass of the game went to **Adonai Mitchell** with less than a minute left. **C.J. Stroud**, who had 4 TD passes of his own, nearly led the Buckeyes back, but a 50-yard field goal try missed on the final play.

Arian Smith of Georgia

Max Duggan hung in against the Michigan D.

National Championship Game

GEORGIA 65, TCU 7

This wasn't a win, it was a rout. The Bulldogs became the first team since 2012 to repeat as national champions. Their victory margin of 58 points was not only the biggest ever in a championship game . . . it was the most in any bowl game—ever! Georgia dominated every part of the game, holding TCU to only 188 yards of offense, and intercepting Heisman Trophy–runner-up **Max Duggan** two times.

Meanwhile, Georgia QB **Stetson Bennett** (below) had a field day. The former walk-on earned his second Championship Game Offensive MVP award by throwing 4 TD passes and running for 2 more. **Branson Robinson** ran for 2 scores to lead the rushing attack. The defense added a fumble recovery and 5 sacks on a day they completely shut down TCU's high-scoring offense. **Javon Bullard** (right) was Defensive MVP for his 2 picks and a fumble recovery.

The Bulldogs finished the season 15–0 after going 14–1 in 2021. With many of its key players back in 2023, will they make it a three-peat?

AP FINAL TOP TEN

1. Georgia	6. Tennessee
2. TCU	7. Penn State
3. Michigan	8. Washington
4. Ohio State	9. Tulane
5. Alabama	10. Utah

WNBA/NBA

REACHING . . .
A'ja Wilson and the Las Vegas Aces soared above the Connecticut Sun to win their first WNBA championship. It was the wrap-up of a great 2022 season that saw women's basketball become more popular than ever. Hoops fans then turned their attention to the NBA . . .

. . . FOR THE SKY!

. . . where the Denver Nuggets matched the Aces with their own first-ever league championship. The Nuggets won it all in their 47th season in the league, knocking off the gutsy Miami Heat in five games. Nikola Jokić led the way with a record series of triple-doubles. Read on for more great stories of the WNBA and NBA.

WNBA 2022

Women's basketball continues to be one of the fastest-growing sports around. In 2022, the WNBA had its best TV ratings in 14 seasons! The All-Star Game and the draft also attracted big audiences. Those fans watched some pretty awesome hoops in 2022; with less than a month left in the season, 11 out of 12 teams still had a shot at a playoff berth. Even with less than a week left, six teams were chasing the final three playoff spots. A new format for the playoffs meant that no team had a first-round bye, but finishing high in the standings was still a big deal and gave those teams home-court advantage.

Two teams both had hot starts to the season. The Las Vegas Aces and Chicago Sky each won 15 of their first 20 games. Led by powerhouse forward **A'ja Wilson**, the Aces kept their success going until the end of the regular season; their 26–10 mark was tied for the league's best with the defending-champion Sky, led by hometown hero **Candace Parker**.

During that early-season run, the two teams met and made history. Playing at home, Las Vegas roared out to a big lead. At one point in the second quarter, they led the Sky by 28 points. But Chicago never quit. Guard **Courtney Vandersloot** led the way with 25 points and

Commissioner's Cup

Like European soccer leagues, the WNBA created an in-season tournament among its teams. Games were played throughout the regular season. The Aces met the Sky in the final, with the Aces winning 93-83. The Cup raised money for charities chosen by each of the 12 teams, while also giving players an additional payday.

Vandersloot's pinpoint passing helped Chicago make a record comeback.

8 assists as the Sky did a little roaring of their own. They made up the difference and ended up winning 104-95. It was the biggest single-game comeback in WNBA history!

Another record-setting performance was put together by **Sabrina Ionescu** of the New York Liberty. She had the second triple-double of her career, just the 11th in league history, in a loss to the Sky. When the season was over, Ionescu was the first WNBA player ever with 500 points, 200 rebounds, and 200 assists in a single season. Talk about doing it all!

The WNBA also said goodbye to two legends. **Sylvia Fowles** wrapped up 15 incredible seasons by winning the league rebounding title for the third time. **Sue Bird** retired after 19 seasons as one of the WNBA's all-time best in assists and three-point shooting. (See pages 27–28 for more on these heroes.)

Once the playoff field was set, two former top teams were on the outside looking in—the Minnesota Lynx and the Los Angeles Sparks. It was the first season since 2010 that the Lynx missed the postseason, while 2022 marked two seasons in a row that the Sparks, a five-time WNBA Finals team, had missed the playoffs.

Of course, once the playoffs began, the records went out the door. For all the exciting action—and to see who ended up on top—flip the page!

WNBA 2022 Awards

MOST VALUABLE PLAYER
DEFENSIVE PLAYER OF THE YEAR
A'ja Wilson, Aces

ROOKIE OF THE YEAR
Rhyne Howard, Dream

MOST IMPROVED PLAYER
Jackie Young, Aces

SIXTH PLAYER
Brionna Jones, Sun

COACH OF THE YEAR
Becky Hammon, Aces

WNBA Stat Champs

(per-game averages, except three-pointer total)

21.8 POINTS
Breanna Stewart, Storm

9.8 REBOUNDS
Sylvia Fowles, Lynx

7.0 ASSISTS
Natasha Cloud, Mystics

1.9 BLOCKS
A'ja Wilson, Aces

113 THREE-POINTERS
Kelsey Plum, Aces

Rhyne Howard

2022 WNBA Playoffs

First Round

Aces 2, Mercury 0

Las Vegas set a WNBA record—regular or postseason—with 23 three-point baskets on the way to a Game 2 117-80 rout of the Mercury. No other team had even reached 20 treys! **Chelsea Gray** had 27 points while **Kelsey Plum** had 22.

Storm 2, Mystics 0

Sue Bird's final season got at least one series longer. The WNBA legend led Seattle to a sweep of Washington. In Game 1, Washington got 26 points from superstar **Elena Delle Donne**, but they were not enough. **Breanna Stewart** led the way for the Storm with 23 points and 12 boards.

Sky 2, Liberty 1

The defending champs from Chicago took a hit in Game 1 as the Liberty pulled off a big upset on the road. Star guard **Sabrina Ionescu** led the way for New York, who scored the last 13 points of the game. However, Chicago bounced back like a champ, winning Game 2 100-62, the biggest victory margin in WNBA postseason history! They also won Game 3 to wrap up the series.

Sun 2, Wings 1

Like Las Vegas, Connecticut reached its fourth straight WNBA semifinals. They had to beat a tough Wings team. In the clinching win, they used defense—forcing 19 turnovers—and rebounding, with 17 offensive boards, to hold off Dallas.

Semifinals

Aces 3, Storm 1

Late scores by Gray when the game was tied clinched the win for Las Vegas. She finished with a career playoff high of 31 points to send the Aces to the WNBA Finals. **A'ja Wilson** was her usual awesome self, with 23 points and 13 rebounds. Even Stewart's 42 points were not enough to keep Seattle's hopes alive.

Sun 3, Sky 2

In the clinching Game 5, Connecticut's defense led the way until the Sun shut out the Sky for almost the final five minutes while outscoring them 10-0. The Sun joined the Aces in a matchup of teams seeking their first WNBA championship.

Candace Parker led Chicago past New York.

2022 WNBA Finals

GAME 1 Aces 67, Sun 64

Las Vegas put up its lowest point total of the entire season but used strong defense to hold off Connecticut. Having the newly crowned WNBA MVP **A'ja Wilson** certainly helped. Wilson had 24 points and 11 rebounds, her fourth straight playoff double-double. It was the first WNBA Finals game win ever for the Aces.

GAME 2 Aces 85, Sun 71

The Aces just had too much Wilson in this game. The WNBA MVP put up yet another double-double. Her 26 points were the most in the game, though **Chelsea Gray** had 21 and **Kelsey Plum** put in 20. After being swept in their two earlier WNBA Finals appearances, the Aces were now just one win away from their first league title.

Even double-teamed, A'ja Wilson powered through, leading Las Vegas to victory.

Las Vegas celebrated its first WNBA championship!

GAME 3 **Sun 105, Aces 76**

Connecticut had to win to stay alive. Thanks to **Alyssa Thomas**, they did. Thomas had the first triple-double in WNBA Finals history (16 points, 15 rebounds, 11 assists). Former MVP **Jonquel Jones** had 20 points, while **DeWanna Bonner** had 18. The Sun's 105 was the most they had ever scored in a WNBA Finals game.

GAME 4 **Aces 78, Sun 71**

Las Vegas won the first WNBA championship in team history, led by Wilson and first-year coach **Becky Hammon**. The Aces scored the last eight points of the game to finish off the hard-working Sun. Gray averaged 18.3 points per game and was named the WNBA Finals MVP. Even another triple-double by Connecticut's Thomas couldn't keep the Aces from grabbing the trophy.

2022 WNBA STANDINGS

1.	**Las Vegas Aces**	26–10
2.	**Chicago Sky**	26–10
3.	**Connecticut Sun**	25–11
4.	**Seattle Storm**	22–14
5.	**Washington Mystics**	22–14
6.	**Dallas Wings**	18–18
7.	**New York Liberty**	16–20
8.	**Phoenix Mercury**	15–21
9.	**Minnesota Lynx**	14–22
10.	**Atlanta Dream**	14–22
11.	**Los Angeles Sparks**	13–23
12.	**Indiana Fever**	5–31

2022-23 NBA

If you were an NBA fan in 2022–23, you were not alone! An all-time record 22.23 million people attended NBA games last season. And 791 of those games were sellouts, also an all-time record. The average of 18,077 fans per game marks the first time that number has gone above 18,000. All of those fans saw a fantastic mix of record-setting scoring, highlight-reel dunking, and surprises from teams on the rise. Scoring was up all over, too. In fact, this season was the first in NBA history in which six players each finished with an average above 30 points per game. Also, players combined for more 30- and 40-point games than in any other season. Fifteen players scored at least 50 points in a game, the most since the incredible, high-scoring **Wilt Chamberlain** played in the early 1960s.

A big story in 2022–23 was the impact of players from outside the United States. It's a story that has been building for a while. Denver's **Nikola Jokić** (Serbia) won the previous two NBA MVP awards. His passing skills are incredible. Milwaukee's **Giannis Antetokounmpo** (Greece) is also a two-time MVP. In one five-game stretch in 2023, he was the first NBA player in a half century to pile up more than 200 points, 80 rebounds, and 30 assists. **Joel Embiid** (Cameroon) of the Philadelphia 76ers won his second NBA scoring title in a row and his first NBA MVP. Four players from outside the US made the All-NBA First Team as well. And the first pick in the 2023 NBA draft was **Victor Wembanyama** (France), taken by the lucky San Antonio Spurs.

American players made more than their share of news, too. Lakers hero **LeBron James** became the NBA's all-

Joel Embiid

time leading scorer (see pages 10 and 93). **Jayson Tatum** led the Celtics to their best win total in 14 seasons. (Tatum also set an NBA All-Star Game record with an incredible 55 points in the midseason points fest.) **Jimmy Butler** led his Miami Heat to the NBA Finals, while **Donovan Mitchell** moved from the Jazz to the Cavaliers and carried them to their first postseason since 2018.

In February, the Phoenix Suns pulled off the biggest trade of the year, snagging megastar **Kevin Durant** from Brooklyn. Durant then led the Suns in scoring in six of his first seven games with them. Along with star guard **Devin Booker**, Durant sent the Suns to the playoffs.

Joining them there in the Western Conference postseason were the Sacramento Kings. Led by **De'Aaron Fox** and **Domantas Sabonis**, "Sacto" earned its first postseason spot since 2006. The Western Conference was packed with great teams, and it took a crazy final day of the regular season to set up the play-in games. LeBron's Lakers beat Minnesota to earn a playoff spot—not bad after starting the season

Fox helped the Kings soar to new heights.

2–10. The Golden State Warriors locked up their spot with a final-game win, scoring 55 points in the first quarter, the most ever to start a game in NBA history.

In the Eastern Conference, the surprise team was the New York Knicks. **Julius Randle** led the way as the team made its second playoff appearance since 2012–13.

Fans added even more sellouts in the playoffs, while the players piled up more highlights. Read on to recap the season and find out who cut down the net as NBA champs in 2023!

Kevin Durant

In the Paint

59 Is Fine: On November 13, Philadelphia's **Joel Embiid** went for 59 points, a career best. But he did more than score. Embiid was the first player since 1976 to have that many points while also topping 10 rebounds, 5 assists, and 5 blocks in a game. The Sixers star wound up as the NBA scoring champ, too.

Mr. Everything: Nikola **Jokić** of the Nuggets can really do it all. He proved it in a win over the Hornets by scoring 40 points, pulling down 27 rebounds, and dishing out 10 assists. He became the third player ever with a 35/25/10 stats line in a game.

Another Mr. Everything: Dallas's **Luka Dončić** did Jokić one better (well, more than one!). Trailing the Knicks in a December game, Dončić missed a free throw on purpose, grabbed the rebound, and made a basket while falling down . . . to tie the game just before the buzzer! In overtime, he scored 7 points to reach 60 and Dallas won 126-121. Want more numbers? Dončić's totals of 60

points, 21 boards, and 10 dimes made him the second-ever 60-point triple-double player. In a late December five-game stretch, Dončić also became the first player to pile up more than 225 points, 50 rebounds, and 50 assists.

*Luka
Dončić*

Busy Scorekeepers:

The folks keeping track of the Kings–Clippers game in February probably burned out their computers. The Kings won 176-175 in the second-highest scoring game in NBA history. Sacramento scored the last seven points of the double-overtime thriller.

71 Was Their Lucky Number:

Cleveland guard **Donovan Mitchell** led his team to the playoffs with great all-around play. But scoring was his main contribution. He put up 71 points in one game! That total is now a Cleveland record, topping the old mark set by **Kyrie Irving** and some guy named **LeBron**. Mitchell wasn't alone. Portland's superstar guard **Damian Lillard** matched Mitchell's 71 in a February game, setting a Trail Blazers team record.

0-13,884

That was the record of NBA teams since 2002 that trailed by nine points with 35 seconds to go in a game. That is, until Dallas and **Luka Dončić** came back to beat the Knicks on December 28, 2022.

The Scoring King

Numbers are pretty amazing. Check these out. **LeBron James** was 38 years old on February 7, 2023, when he made a short jumper against the Thunder that gave him 38,388 points for his career. That broke the all-time NBA career scoring record set by **Kareem Abdul-Jabbar**, who scored his final NBA points in 1989. How many points did James finish with on his historic night? That's right: 38. "The King" is now "The Scoring King," cementing his spot as a basketball GOAT. James finished the 2022–23 season with 38,652 points . . . with more to come!

NBA Playoffs

Play-In Tournament

→ The Lakers earned a spot with an overtime win over the Timberwolves.

→ The Chicago Bulls became the first 10-seed to earn a spot in the playoffs after they beat **Trae Young** and the Hawks.

Playoff Highlights

→ No. 8 seed Miami shocked the top-seeded Milwaukee Bucks. The Heat's **Jimmy Butler** averaged 37.6 points per game in the five-game win.

→ **Stephen Curry** became the first player ever to score 50 points in a Game 7 to lead Golden State over Sacramento.

→ Led by "The King," **LeBron James**, the Lakers romped past the No. 2-seeded Memphis Grizzlies, winning the series-clinching Game 6 by 40 points!

→ Miami kept up its upset streak. In the conference semifinals, they beat the Knicks, becoming the second No. 8 seed ever to reach the conference finals.

Curry set a short-lived scoring record.

→ Denver's **Nikola Jokić** had three triple-doubles as his Nuggets beat the Suns in six games.

→ Boston's **Jayson Tatum** broke Curry's two-week-old record with 51 points as the Celtics sent the Sixers home in Game 7.

CONFERENCE FINALS

Eastern Conference
HEAT 4, CELTICS 3

Miami breathed a sigh of relief after dominating Boston in Game 7, winning by 19 points. That sent them to their seventh NBA Finals, but the first by a No. 8 seed since 1999. Miami had won the first three games of the series rather easily, but Boston stormed back. In Game 6, **Derrick White** tipped in a basket with 0.2 seconds left to force a Game 7. No NBA team has ever come back from being down 3-0 to win . . . but the Celtics couldn't make history, even though the game was at home. Miami star **Jimmy Butler** had 28 points in Game 7 to lead the way.

Western Conference
NUGGETS 4, LAKERS 0

Nikola Jokić continued his awesome play, racking up three triple-doubles as the Nuggets swept the Lakers. Denver headed to its first-ever NBA Finals. **Jamal Murray**'s lights-out shooting led to a Game 2 Denver win. The Nuggets offense put together a strong fourth quarter to win Game 3. Denver's **Aaron Gordon** blocked a **LeBron James** shot near the end of Game 4 to seal the series win.

White's tip-in gave the Celtics life.

NBA Finals

History was going to be made no matter who won the 2023 NBA Finals. Either the Denver Nuggets would win their first championship ever . . . or the Miami Heat would become the first No. 8 seed to claim the title. Let's see what happened!

GAME 1
NUGGETS 104, HEAT 93

Nikola Jokić continued his hot playoffs with another triple-double, including 27 points. Teammate **Jamal Murray** poured in 26 points to back him up. **Bam Adebayo** was tops for Miami with 26 points of his own. The Heat trailed by 21 points entering the fourth quarter. They outscored the Nuggets in that final period, but their comeback fell short.

GAME 2
HEAT 111, NUGGETS 108

Miami stormed from behind again, but this time ended up on top. The Heat outscored the Nuggets by 11 points in the final quarter, led by **Jimmy Butler**'s 21 total points in the game. Backup **Gabe Vincent** surprised everyone by leading Miami with 23 points. Jokić continued his hot play with a game-high 41 points, but it was not enough.

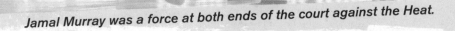

Jamal Murray was a force at both ends of the court against the Heat.

HISTORIC MVP

Nikola Jokić took home the Bill Russell Trophy as the MVP of the NBA Finals. It was an easy choice. He was the first ever to lead all players in points, assists, and rebounds in a single postseason. The native of Serbia has dominated since coming to the NBA in 2015. He was the league MVP in 2021 and 2022. After getting his Russell Award, though, he said it was a bigger deal than those. "We are not in it for ourselves, we are in it for the guy next to us," Jokić said.

GAME 3
NUGGETS 109, HEAT 94

Jokić and Murray became the first teammates ever to both have 30-point triple-doubles in an NBA playoff game. Their 1-2 combination was too much for the Heat. Jokić added an incredible 21 rebounds to his 32 points, while Murray had 10 assists to go along with 34 points. Butler scored 28 for the Heat but didn't get enough help from his teammates.

GAME 4
NUGGETS 108, HEAT 95

Denver found another star in **Aaron Gordon**, who led his team with 27 points while the Heat bottled up Jokić and Murray (sort of . . . Jokić still had 23 points!). Another lesser-known Nuggets player, **Bruce Brown Jr.**, contributed 21 points. Miami had six players with at least 10 points, led by Butler's 25.

GAME 5
NUGGETS 94, HEAT 89

The Nuggets won their first-ever NBA title with a scrappy victory in front of a home crowd in Denver. Jokić led the way with 28 points and 16 rebounds. Denver outscored Miami in the second half 50-38, although Miami did hold the lead late in the fourth quarter. A key three-point basket by **Kontavious Caldwell-Pope** and clutch free throws by him and Brown sealed the win.

2022-23 Stat Leaders

(per-game averages, except for three-pointer total)

33.1 POINTS
Joel Embiid
76ERS

12.3 REBOUNDS
Domantas Sabonis
KINGS

10.7 ASSISTS
James Harden ▶▶▶
76ERS

1.9 STEALS
O. G. Anunoby
RAPTORS

301 THREE-POINTERS
Klay Thompson
WARRIORS

3.0 BLOCKS
Jaren Jackson Jr.
GRIZZLIES

2022-23 NBA Awards

MOST VALUABLE PLAYER
JOEL EMBIID
76ERS

DEFENSIVE PLAYER OF THE YEAR
JAREN JACKSON JR.
GRIZZLIES

ROOKIE OF THE YEAR
PAOLO BANCHERO ▶▶▶
MAGIC

MOST IMPROVED PLAYER
LAURI MARKKANEN
JAZZ

CLUTCH PLAYER OF THE YEAR
DE'AARON FOX
KINGS

SIXTH MAN
MALCOLM BROGDON
CELTICS

COACH OF THE YEAR
MIKE BROWN
KINGS

COLLEGE BASKETBALL

DOMINANT CHAMP
Connecticut won its third men's national championship with a dominant run through the tournament. It won six games in a row by at least 10 points. In the final (where Jordan Hawkins slammed this basket home), it wrapped things up with a 76-59 win over San Diego State, making its first title-game appearance ever. Find out more about a busy men's season and a wild tournament in this chapter!

BRAND-NEW CHAMP
LSU had come very close in the past, reaching the Final Four five times. Not until 2023, however, did they end up as the champion. The Tigers put on an offensive show in the championship game, wiping out Iowa 102-85. Here, Taylor Soule scores two of the points that helped LSU set a women's title-game scoring record! For more on the women's season, including some record-setting performances, keep reading!

2022-23 NCAA Hoops

Antoine Davis

Has women's college hoops ever been more popular? Probably not! The 2022–23 season saw a big rise in attention and ratings for a game that is packed with talent. Want proof? The attendance record for the NCAA Women's Basketball tournament was shattered throughout nearly every round, with the peak coming during the regional finals. Those four games brought in 82,275 fans, beating the previous record by nearly 10,000! (That record was also 20 years old!) During the season, one historic scoring record fell, and another came very close. Oklahoma's **Taylor Robertson** broke the NCAA Division I three-point record when she drained her 498th career shot from beyond the arc. The mark had previously been held by Ohio State's **Kelsey Mitchell**. After Robertson's Sooners season ended, her record to beat is 537 "treys."

Taylor Robertson

On the men's side, Louisiana State legend **Pete Maravich**'s career scoring record of 3,667 points has stood for more than 50 years. In 2023, Detroit Mercy's **Antoine Davis** made a pretty good run at topping that mark. He was seven points shy after his team's last regular-season game. Unfortunately, their 14–19 record did not earn a playoff spot, and Davis ended up second all-time. Still, he did lead the nation in scoring average at 28.2 points per game.

Once the men's NCAA tournament began, fans saw just how deep the talent pool is in hoops. For the first time in tournament history, not a single No. 1 seed made it past the Sweet Sixteen. In fact, by the end of the first round, not a single perfect bracket remained out of the tens of millions filled out online. (A big reason, of course, was surprise No. 16 winner Farleigh Dickinson University.) The women's tournament also saw some upsets, plus the rise of some new basketball powers.

As both tournaments went on, more and more Cinderellas saw the shoe fit. The women's event ended with a brand-new champ, while the men's Final Four featured three teams that had never been there before. College basketball continues to get more and more exciting; what will the new season bring?!

Zach Edey

TOP PLAYERS

WOODEN AND NAISMITH AWARDS

Caitlin Clark, IOWA (PAGE 114)
Zach Edey, PURDUE

FINAL MEN'S TOP 10
(CBS Sports)
1. Connecticut
2. San Diego State
3. Miami
4. Alabama
5. FAU
6. Houston
7. Texas
8. UCLA
9. Kansas State
10. Gonzaga

FINAL WOMEN'S TOP 10
(USA Today)
1. LSU
2. Iowa
3. South Carolina
4. Virginia Tech
5. Maryland
6. Ohio State
7. Indiana
8. Utah
9. Connecticut
10. Stanford

Colin Castleton and Florida surprised No. 2 Tennessee in one of the year's big upsets.

Men's Highlights

Home Court Disadvantage:
On January 19, Gonzaga had their 76-game home winning streak snapped in a shocking upset by Loyola Marymount 68-67. It was the first time Gonzaga had lost in "The Kennel" since 2018, nearly five years. (Why the funny arena nickname? Well, the school's team nickname is the Bulldogs, after all!) After the upset, the next-longest home winning streak in men's college basketball was Auburn's at 28. Six days after Gonzaga's loss, however, Auburn fell at home to Texas A&M 79-63.

Terrible 2s:
Several top teams lost throughout the regular season, but the one that set a record was No. 2 Tennessee. When the Volunteers lost to unranked Florida 67-54, they became the 10th different top-2 team to lose during the year. That's the most in the history of the Associated Press poll.

Biggest Upset?:
College basketball seasons are always filled with upsets. One that will be remembered from 2022–23 came in a January Big East matchup. No. 6 Connecticut

played unranked St. John's. The Red Storm surprised the Huskies by tying the game 38-38 at halftime. But then St. John's held on to win 85-74. It was the first time the school had beaten a top-6 team in five years. The loss must have woken up the Huskies. They won 15 of their next 17 . . . and went on to win the national title!

Revolving Door at the Top:

Want more evidence that 2022–23 was a topsy-turvy year? After UNC spent the first three weeks as the No. 1 team, Houston was the next team to claim the top spot. But then it lost to No. 8 Alabama 71-65 on December 10. Next up on top was Purdue. They were No. 1 for four weeks until losing to unranked Rutgers on January 2 on their home court. In a season that didn't really see a dominant team, by the end of the regular season, Houston and Purdue had held the No. 1 ranking for seven weeks each. Along with UNC, Alabama also rose to the top twice and led the final poll leading up to the tournament.

It's Not How You Start: The

North Carolina Tar Heels were ranked as the preseason No. 1 team after reaching the 2022 championship game. However, they didn't live up to the hype. UNC went 11–9 during ACC play, then lost in the ACC tournament. The legendary hoops school became the first preseason No. 1 to miss the national tournament since the tournament expanded in 1985.

Rutgers rose to upset No. 1 Purdue.

Women's Highlights

Title Game Preview?: Well, no, as it turned out. When No. 1 South Carolina and No. 2 Stanford met on November 20, it was a matchup of the sport's two most recent champions. Many hoped the pair would end up in the title game, too. This regular-season battle ended up being only the third 1 vs. 2 game in history to go to overtime. The Gamecocks beat the Cardinal 76-71. The game would have ended with Stanford on top in regulation if not for South Carolina superstar Aliyah Boston, who tied the game with only 2.1 seconds left. Boston ended the night with 14 points and 13 rebounds.

Historic Back-to-Back:

Connecticut has been one of the top women's hoops programs for decades. But in February 2023, they did something they had not done since 1993—lost back-to-back games! After falling to No. 1 South Carolina, the Huskies lost to Marquette to break that very impressive streak.

Superstar Aliyah Boston led South Carolina to a big early-season win over Stanford.

Don't Rank Us No. 2:

That's what Stanford was saying midseason. In January, they were No. 2 when they were upset by Pac-12 rival USC, which was unranked. In February, Stanford had made it back to No. 2 . . . but then lost another Pac-12 game to Washington!

SEC Must-See: One of the

biggest SEC regular-season games in decades took place on February 12 in South Carolina. No. 1 South Carolina played host to No. 3 LSU in the first top-3 SEC matchup since 1990. As LSU head coach **Kim Mulkey** said after the game, "It's South Carolina, in my opinion, and it's everybody else." This came after the Gamecocks handled the Tigers with ease, ultimately winning their 31st consecutive game 88-64. If you feel bad for Mulkey, don't worry, she had herself an okay March.

Maddy Siegrist was the national scoring champ.

Maddy Buckets: Villanova senior

Maddy Siegrist made her presence felt in 2021–22 when she finished as the nation's second-leading scorer (27.8 points per game). This season, Siegrist put her name at the top of the nation's leaderboard. By year's end, Siegrist averaged 29.2 ppg, finishing ahead of Iowa's **Caitlin Clark** (27.8 ppg) to win the national scoring title. Against Creighton, Siegrist made Villanova history, too, when she scored her 2,409th point, the most career points in school history. By the end of the season, her 2,896 points topped the school's men's record, too! For good measure, Siegrist also graduated with the Big East Conference points record of 1,693 points.

Men's Tournament Highlights

FDU VS. THE WORLD

Fairleigh Dickinson (FDU) didn't even win their conference tournament! The 19–15 Knights lost to Merrimack in the Northeast Conference Championship game on March 7. Still, FDU received a bid into the 64-team tournament by winning a First Four game against Texas Southern. Then, in the definition of a bracket buster, FDU became only the second 16-seed to defeat a No. 1. They beat Purdue 63-58 to make the next round for the first time in school history.

ROARING TIGERS

FDU wasn't the only major upset early, as No. 15 Princeton broke the hearts of No. 2 Arizona 59-55 in the first round. The Tigers didn't stop there, beating No. 7

FAU's Dusty May got a confetti shower.

Zach Martini helped in Princeton's upset.

Missouri 78-65. That win over Missouri was the Ivy League's first tournament win over an SEC opponent since 1942!

ONE IS THE LONELIEST NUMBER

For the first time ever, by the end of the Sweet Sixteen, not a single No. 1 seed had survived. Along with Purdue's loss (page 109), No. 1 Kansas lost to No. 8 Arkansas in the Round of 32, 72-71. In the Sweet Sixteen, both No. 1 Alabama and No. 1 Houston fell. At least Alabama and Houston both lost to Final Four teams, San Diego State and Miami.

Grant Singleton (right) and FDU pulled off the tournament's biggest shocker!

FIRST TIME FOR EVERYTHING AND EVERYONE

For the first time since 1970, three teams made their first appearance in the Final Four, and for the first time ever, no top-3 seed made it either! No. 5 San Diego State won the South Regional Final over No. 6 Creighton by one point on a last-second free throw. No. 5 Miami defeated No. 2 Texas in the Midwest Regional Final 88-81. And No. 4 Connecticut beat No. 3 Gonzaga in a 82-54 blowout in the West Regional Final. The most surprising participant, at the end of the day, however, was No. 9 Florida Atlantic. FAU had never won an NCAA tournament game before this year. They then defeated No. 8 Memphis, No. 16 FDU, No. 4 Tennessee, and No. 3 Kansas State to make it to the Final Four. FAU made such an impression on Kansas State head coach **Jerome Tang** that he actually made his way over to the Owls' locker room postgame, telling FAU they were "the toughest [team] that we played all year long."

Men's Final Four

Connecticut 72, Miami 59

UConn was the only program with Final Four experience coming into the tournament's final days. They sure looked like it in this game. The Huskies defeated the Hurricanes by 13 points, which is pretty good, but it was also the closest winning margin for UConn in the tournament so far! In beating Miami by double digits, UConn became only the sixth team since the 64-team expansion to enter the championship game with five double-digit victories. **Adama Sanogo** led the Huskies with 21 points and 10 rebounds, and **Jordan Hawkins** added 13 points while battling flu-like symptoms.

San Diego State 72, FAU 71

Junior **Lamont Butler** became a March Madness legend when he made a buzzer-beating jumper to send the Aztecs to their first NCAA championship game in program history! Butler's shot became the tournament's most talked-about moment and immediately went down as one of the most historic shots of all time. In fact, Butler's game-winner was the first buzzer beater while trailing in Final Four history! Senior **Matt Bradley** led San Diego State in the semifinal with 21 points.

Lamont Butler was hugged by his team!

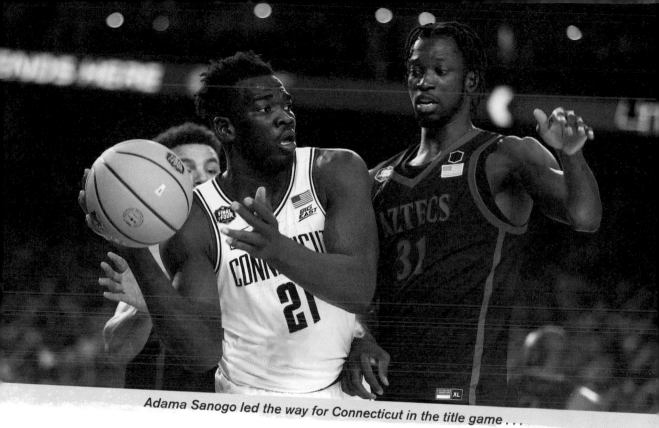

Adama Sanogo led the way for Connecticut in the title game . . .

Championship Game

Connecticut 76, San Diego State 59

Capping one of the most dominant runs in tournament history, the Huskies would not be denied. They won the title with a sixth double-digit victory. The win gave the Huskies their fifth championship in program history. The No. 4 Huskies became only the third 3-seed or lower to win the tournament in the last 15 years, joining . . . themselves! In 2014, UConn won it all as a 7-seed, after taking home the crown as a 3-seed in 2011. Head coach **Dan Hurley** became the third coach in program history to win a national title, joining **Jim Calhoun** and **Kevin Ollie**. **Adama Sanogo**, who collected 17 points and

10 rebounds during the title game, was named the NCAA Final Four Most Outstanding Player.

. . . and then joyfully cut down the net!

Women's Tournament Highlights

IF A TREE FALLS IN A FOREST

Remember how back in November people wondered if that South Carolina vs. Stanford matchup would be a Final Four preview? Well, in the second round of the NCAA tournament, No. 8 Mississippi made sure that wouldn't happen. Ole Miss knocked off No. 1 Stanford 54-49. The upset gave the Rebels their 11th Sweet Sixteen berth in program history, and was the first time they'd ever knocked off a top seed.

12 VS. 5 x 2!

Every season, when picking brackets for these tournaments, fans always look for the 12 vs. 5 matchups. They always seem to be the site of upsets, and 2023 was no different. No. 12 Toledo shocked No. 5 Iowa State 80-73, while Florida Gulf Coast, also a 12-seed, did the same to No. 5 Washington State 74-63. Unfortunately, both winners lost in the second round.

Destiny Harden

YEAR OF THE U

Stanford wasn't the only No. 1 seed to go down in the second round. With 3.3 seconds left between No. 9 Miami and No. 1 Indiana, **Destiny Harden** hit a short jumper to send Miami to the Sweet Sixteen! It was only the third time in tournament history that a No. 9 had knocked off a No. 1. The Hurricanes advanced to their first Sweet Sixteen since 1992, and "The U" did not stop there. They also upset No. 4 Villanova to advance to their first-ever Elite Eight. Miami became the first school to have both their men's and women's teams advance to the Elite Eight in the same year, with neither team being a top-4 seed.

THE INCREDIBLE CLARK

After watching Iowa's all-around superstar **Caitlin Clark** do her stuff for two seasons, you'd think fans would not be surprised by her. But in a stunning

97-83 win over Louisville, Clark made history again. She scored 41 points, had 12 assists, and grabbed 10 rebounds. That gave her the first 40-point (or even 30-point!) triple-double in NCAA tournament history, for men or women. Among her other accomplishments, she also set new tournament records, with 191 total points and 60 total assists. During the regular season, she was the first women's player ever with more than 1,000 points *and* 300 assists in a single season. Though her season didn't end by cutting down the nets, Clark has another chance in 2024, as she will be back for another season.

LAST FOUR STANDING

As expected, top-seeded South Carolina reached its third consecutive Final Four, as the Gamecocks defeated No. 2 Maryland 86-75 to win their 42nd game in a row. No. 1 Virginia Tech also took care of business, defeating No. 3 Ohio State 84-74 to advance to the first Final Four in program history. In the West, Iowa's Clark led the Hawkeyes to their first Final Four since 1993 with that historic 41-point triple-double. Rounding out the Final Four, coach **Kim Mulkey**'s LSU Tigers beat No. 9 Miami 54-42.

Virginia Tech players and coaches show how many teams are left in the NCAA tournament.

Women's Final Four

Caitlin Clark doing what she does best!

Iowa 77, South Carolina 73

Caitlin Clark! After dropping 41 points in the Elite Eight, Clark became the first player in tournament history to record back-to-back 40-point games. She poured in 41 more as her Hawkeyes defeated top-seeded South Carolina. It was SC's first loss in 43 games! The win advanced the Hawkeyes to their first championship game in program history, and was also the Hawkeyes' first-ever win over a top-seeded opponent!

LSU 79, Virginia Tech 72

The sixth time's the charm! LSU went to five straight Final Fours from 2004 through 2008. However, they never made it past the semifinal. But a fourth-quarter comeback led the Tigers to their first title game in program history. After entering the final quarter down 59-50, LSU erupted, outscoring Virginia Tech 29-13 to earn a spot in the tournament's final game. "I came here for lots of reasons," said LSU head coach Kim Mulkey, who had previously won three titles at Baylor. "One was to someday hang a championship banner at LSU."

Championship Game

LSU 102, Iowa 85

Coach Mulkey got what she came for two days later. Her Tigers put on a bucket-filling show, setting a record for most points scored in a women's Final Four game. It was all hands on deck for the Tigers. **Jasmine Carson** hadn't made a shot since the tournament's second round. Then, in the title game, Carson made her first seven shots and had 22 points by halftime!

LSU's star sophomore **Angel Reese** scored 15 points in the final and was named the NCAA Final Four Most Outstanding Player. In only her second year as LSU's head coach, Mulkey delivered. The year before she took over, the Tigers posted a 9–13 record. In 2022–23, LSU went 34–2, and they hung up their new national championship banner at home on opening night when the 2023–24 season began.

LSU's Angel Reese led her team from behind to win the national championship.

A NEW CHAMP IS KNIGHTED

The Vegas Golden Knights won their first Stanley Cup championship, defeating the Florida Panthers in four out of five games. It was only the Knights' sixth season in the league; they joined as an expansion team in 2017. Their rapid rise to the top was not the only big story of the 2022–23 season. Read on for lots more hockey news!

NHL 2022-23

As a generation of stars wind down their NHL careers, a surge of great young players is rising to the top. They are showing off more speed and skills and wild plays than the game has ever seen. Players 25 and under are bringing it! Some are defensemen: **Cale Makar** (Colorado Avalanche), **Adam Fox** (New York Rangers), **Miro Heiskanen** (Dallas Stars), and **Rasmus Dahlin** (Buffalo Sabres). Young stars at forward include **Jack Hughes** (New Jersey Devils), **Jason Robertson** (Stars), **Andrei Svechnikov** (Carolina Hurricanes), **Nick Suzuki** (Montreal Canadiens), **Trevor Zegras** (Anaheim Ducks), **Matty Beniers** (Seattle Kraken), and **Elias Pettersson** (Vancouver Canucks).

Just outside the 25-age group is the league's best player. Edmonton Oilers forward, **Connor McDavid**, at age 26, became just the sixth player in NHL history to have a 150-point season. He was also just the fifth player to lead the league solo in goals, assists, and points during a single season. (The last person to do that was **Wayne "The Great One" Gretzky** in 1987.) Also, McDavid's teammate, **Leon Draisaitl** (who is 27), was second in the league with 128 points!

These young players are sparking a change in which teams are on top, too. For the first time in NHL history, two teams improved by more than 40 points over the previous season: the Devils (+49) and the Kraken (+40).

David Pastrňák of the record-setting Bruins

Ovechkin is eyeing a record of his own!

Veteran players still scored some milestones. **Erik Karlsson** of the San Jose Sharks became the first defenseman in 31 years to score more than 100 points in a single season—and at age 32, the oldest. On April 10, 2023, both **Claude Giroux** (Ottawa Senators) and **Joe Pavelski** (Stars) reached 1,000 points in their careers. And **Alex Ovechkin** of the Washington Capitals had a record-setting 13th 40-goal season, while becoming the third player in NHL history to score 800 career goals. Ovechkin moved past **Gordie Howe** into second on the NHL's all-time goals list.

As a team, the Boston Bruins marched into history by winning 65 games and notching 135 points—the most by a team in a single season. They opened with 14 straight wins at home, and were in first place in the Atlantic Division from start to finish.

The Stanley Cup itself also marched into history when **Nazem Kadri** took it to a mosque for the first time. Kadri was a member of the 2022 Stanley Cup–winning Avalanche. Each player on the championship team gets to spend a day with the Cup. Kadri's family immigrated to Canada from Lebanon and attend a mosque in London, Ontario.

How did this great 2022–23 season end up? Who got to take the Stanley Cup on new adventures? Read on to find out!

2022-23 FINAL STANDINGS

EASTERN CONFERENCE		WESTERN CONFERENCE	
METROPOLITAN DIV.		**CENTRAL DIVISION**	
HURRICANES	113	AVALANCHE	109
DEVILS	112	STARS	108
RANGERS	107	WILD	103
ISLANDERS	93	JETS	95
PENGUINS	91	PREDATORS	92
CAPITALS	80	BLUES	81
FLYERS	75	COYOTES	70
BLUE JACKETS	59	BLACKHAWKS	59
ATLANTIC DIVISION		**PACIFIC DIVISION**	
BRUINS	135	GOLDEN KNIGHTS	111
MAPLE LEAFS	111	OILERS	109
LIGHTNING	98	KINGS	104
PANTHERS	92	KRAKEN	100
SABRES	91	FLAMES	93
SENATORS	86	CANUCKS	83
RED WINGS	80	SHARKS	60
CANADIENS	68	DUCKS	58

Stanley Cup Playoffs

There were some new faces competing for the Stanley Cup. In: The Devils returned after five seasons away, and the Kraken made their debut. Out: The Pittsburgh Penguins' 16-year playoff streak ended, and the Capitals finished out of the running.

Shocking upsets set the stage for playoff thrills. Five teams that had finished with more than 100 points were sent home in the first round. There were also overtime battles—including four extra periods in a Panthers–Hurricanes game (that's like playing more than a full extra game)! The excitement ended in a final between two teams that had never won a Stanley Cup.

What an Upset!

The Florida Panthers made the playoffs on almost the last day of the season. Their first opponent, the Bruins, finished 43 points ahead of them. The Bruins took a commanding 3–1 series lead, but the Panthers clawed their way back to force a series-deciding Game 7. Down by a goal with a minute left in the game, Florida's **Brandon Montour** snapped home a shot to send the game to overtime. Center **Carter Verhaeghe** zipped the puck by Bruins' goalie **Jeremy Swayman** for the series-winning goal in a colossal upset. They proved cats have many lives.

Down Go the Champs!

The 2022 Stanley Cup champion Avalanche were upset by a first-time playoff team, the Seattle Kraken. Seattle Kraken goaltender **Philipp Grubauer** stopped 34 shots in the opening game, for the team's first playoff win ever. In Game 7, Grubauer stopped 33 shots, while forward **Oliver Bjorkstrand** scored both goals in a 2-1 win. The Kraken became the first expansion team to beat the Stanley Cup champs in their first-ever playoff series. Good start!

Grubauer was awesome for the Kraken.

McDavid Not Enough

The Oilers, led by superstars **Connor McDavid** and **Leon Draisaitl**, faced off against the Las Vegas Golden Knights. In Game 1, Draisaitl scored four goals, but the Knights' **Ivan Barbashev** had two of his own in a Las Vegas 6-4 win. McDavid and Las Vegas's **Jonathan Marchessault** and **Jack Eichel** all notched key goals. Marchessault put an exclamation point on the series by scoring a hat trick in a Game 6 5-2 victory.

Florida star Matthew Tkachuk celebrates a goal during his team's sweep of Carolina.

Eastern Conference Final

Florida Panthers 4, Carolina Hurricanes 0
The Hurricanes finished with the league's second-best record, 21 points ahead of the Panthers. But led by forward **Matthew Tkachuk** and ace goaltender **Sergei Bobrovsky**, the Panthers were hardly pussycats. They proved it in an epic 4-overtime Game 1 victory. That set the stage for a nail-biting series where each game was decided by one goal. Bobrovsky was awesome in a Game 3 32-save shutout win. The super-loud Hurricanes fans did their best, but Tkachuk scored the series-clinching goal with 4.9 seconds in Game 4. Florida headed to its second Stanley Cup Final.

Western Conference Final

Las Vegas Golden Knights 4, Dallas Stars 2
Veteran skill and youthful flash were on display in a tough battle between the Golden Knights and the Stars. Dallas's lineup featured young stars **Jason Robertson** and **Miro Heiskanen**. Las Vegas had its own scoring threat in **Jack Eichel**, plus some top veterans. Las Vegas won the first two games in overtime. Dallas lost their cool in Game 3; captain **Jamie Benn** was ejected and his team melted down without him. The Stars were shut out by Las Vegas goaltender **Adin Hill**. Dallas rallied to win the next two games, but Las Vegas closed out the series with a smothering 6-0 win.

Stanley Cup Final

GAME 1

Las Vegas 5, Florida 2

The Golden Knights returned to the Final after a 2018 appearance. Six of the same players from that season were still on the team—a group known as the Golden Misfits. The Panthers returned to the Final after a 26-year absence. With the game tied after two periods, Las Vegas exploded for three goals, including defenseman **Zach Whitecloud**'s game-winner.

GAME 2

Las Vegas 7, Florida 2

After four straight Las Vegas goals in the first two periods, Panthers goaltender **Sergei Bobrovsky** was replaced by

Hill made many great saves for Vegas.

Alex Lyon. It didn't help. Las Vegas poured it on, taking a 6-1 lead. The game got nasty after **Matthew Tkachuk** leveled **Jack Eichel** with a hard but clean hit. Fights broke out and Tkachuk and Las Vegas's **Ivan Barbashev** received penalties.

GAME 3

Florida 3, Las Vegas 2 (OT)

Las Vegas learned that a cornered cat can be dangerous. The Panthers opened the scoring on a **Brandon Montour** goal. Las Vegas answered on the power play when **Mark Stone** tipped in a shot from Marchessault. The Knights then grabbed the lead on another power play goal as Marchessault wristed home a pass from Eichel. Tkachuk sent the game into overtime by deflecting a loose puck home with less than two minutes remaining. **Carter Verhaeghe** flicked a shot over **Adin Hill**'s shoulder less than five minutes into OT, giving Florida its first Stanley Cup Final win in team history.

GAME 4

Las Vegas 3, Florida 2

Las Vegas forward **Chandler Stephenson** silenced the Florida crowd by snapping a shot through Bobrovsky's legs 1:39 into the game. He dug the Panthers into a deeper hole when he blasted his second goal over Bobrovsky's glove early in the second period. **William Karlsson** buried a rebound to give Las Vegas a 3-0 lead. But five minutes later Montour's caroming shot bounced by Hill to get the Panthers on the scoreboard. **Aleksander**

Barkov's goal in the early third period cut the Las Vegas lead to one goal. Once again, with seconds remaining, Tkachuk was in the thick of the action and snapped a shot toward the net, looking to send the game to OT. But Hill kicked out his leg and made a miraculous save to end it.

GAME 5

Las Vegas 9, Florida 3

Golden Knights captain Stone scored a shorthanded goal on a dazzling move in the first period, and his team never looked back. He added two more later to have the first Stanley Cup–clinching hat trick since 1922! After an explosive 4-goal second period, Las Vegas's victory was assured. As the home fans cheered wildly, Stone became the first Knight ever to pick up the winning Cup. It was then handed off, one by one, to his fellow Misfits, before the rest of the team held the Cup high to celebrate their victory.

CONN SMYTHE TROPHY

Jonathan Marchessault of Las Vegas (one of the Misfits) won the Conn Smythe Trophy for best playoff performance. He led all players with 13 goals, many of them game-changers, and added 12 assists. It was quite a feat for a player who was undrafted—until he joined the Florida Panthers! The Panthers let him go in the 2017 expansion draft, when he was chosen by Las Vegas.

MVP Marchessault buries this key goal.

2023 NHL Stat Champs

153 POINTS
64 GOALS
89 ASSISTS
Connor McDavid, Oilers ▶▶▶

101 POINTS (DEFENSE)
Erik Karlsson, Sharks

+49 PLUS-MINUS
Hampus Lindholm, Bruins

1.89 GOALS AGAINST AVG.
.938 SAVE PCT.
Linus Ullmark, Bruins

6 SHUTOUTS
Ilya Sorokin, Islanders

2023 NHL Awards

Hart Trophy
NHL MVP
Ted Lindsay Award
MVP (VOTED BY PLAYERS)
CONNOR MCDAVID, OILERS

Norris Trophy
BEST DEFENSEMAN
ERIK KARLSSON, SHARKS

Vezina Trophy
BEST GOALIE
LINUS ULLMARK, BRUINS

Calder Trophy
BEST ROOKIE
MATTY BENIERS, KRAKEN

Selke Trophy
BEST DEFENSIVE FORWARD
PATRICE BERGERON, BRUINS

Lady Byng Trophy
SPORTSMANSHIP
ANZE KOPITAR, KINGS ▶▶▶

Masterton Trophy
PERSEVERANCE AND DEDICATION TO HOCKEY
KRIS LETANG, PENGUINS

Mark Messier Leadership Award
STEVEN STAMKOS, LIGHTNING

Jack Adams Award
TOP COACH
JIM MONTGOMERY, BRUINS

Premier Hockey Federation

Forward **Michela Cava** scored 3 goals and added 3 assists (2 of which came on her birthday, March 26!) to help push the Toronto Six to the 2023 Isobel Cup, the championship of the Premier Hockey Federation (PHF). The Thunder Bay, Ontario, native helped her team beat the Minnesota Whitecaps to become the first Canadian team to win the Cup, and Cava was named playoffs MVP.

The final was a one-game playoff in the Arizona Coyotes' arena in Tempe. The T6 were trailing 3-2 in the third period when forward **Taylor Woods** got the tying goal off a pass from Cava. Then **Tereza Vanišová**, a forward who also plays on the Czech national team, scored the winning goal in overtime, which is played three-on-three.

The PHF was founded in 2015 to inspire women and girls to play hockey and to give elite female players the opportunity to earn a living playing the sport they love. It currently has seven teams—the Buffalo Beauts, Boston Pride, Metropolitan (NY) Riveters, Minnesota Whitecaps, Connecticut Whale, Montreal Force, and Toronto Six—that each play a 24-game schedule.

The Isobel Cup is named for **Isobel Gathorne-Hardy**, Lord Frederick Arthur Stanley's daughter, who was one of the first female ice hockey players in Canada.

Michela Cava

This one's about to go in! Hilary Knight led the way for the US National Team.

International Hockey

US Women's National Team

On April 16 in Brampton, Ontario, in front of a crowd wildly cheering for Team Canada, the US Women's National Hockey Team won gold, defeating their northern rivals 6-3 to win their tenth IIHF Women's World Championship.

Forward **Hilary Knight** scored a hat trick in the game; the third goal came late in the last period and was the game-winner. Knight also led the tournament with 8 goals. Team captain Knight, on the team since 2006, called the US team the underdogs heading into the championship game, because Canada won the gold medal the previous two times these nations met.

The teams traded the lead throughout the tough, physical game, until the United States capitalized on two power plays late in the third period to make it 5-3 with less than three minutes remaining. An empty-net goal sealed the comeback victory.

After the tournament, Knight was named the very first International Ice Hockey Federation Female Player of the Year.

MEN'S UNDER-18 CHAMPIONSHIP Two undefeated teams squared off in the 2023 IIHF World Men's Under-18 Championship in Basel, Switzerland, on April 30. After two periods, Sweden was ahead of the United States 2-0. But halfway through the third period, forward **Danny Nelson** scored a goal. Then, with just 3:16 remaining, forwards **Cole Eiserman** and **Carey Terrance** teamed up to tie the score. The US team killed a tough penalty, and **Ryan Leonard** scored 2:20 into overtime to win the game.

Will Smith was named MVP for 2023. He had an assist on Terrance's game-tying goal, matching **Jack Hughes**'s 2019 US single-tournament points record.

SOCCER

DREAM COME TRUE

Argentina's Lionel Messi kissed the World Cup while holding his Golden Ball trophy as the tournament's top player. The ceremony capped off the most exciting day in World Cup history, with Argentina beating France 4-2 on penalty kicks after a thrilling, back-and-forth, extra-time 3-3 tie. Billions of people around the world shared the joy of watching such a tremendous game. It was just one of the many highlights of the past year in soccer!

The best goal of the tournament was scored by Brazil's Richarlison. He took a pass from Vinícius Júnior off his left foot, bounced it into the air, then swept his right leg up and around for a scissor-kick golazo that had fans on their feet!

2022 Men's World Cup

Wow! By the time you read this, about a year has passed since the World Cup in Qatar. And if you're like most soccer fans, you're still tingling from watching **Lionel Messi** and Argentina play **Kylian Mbappé** and France in one of the greatest sporting events ever! The two superstars carried their teams through 120 minutes of nail-biting action. Messi scored two goals; Mbappé scored three (only the second man ever to do so in a World Cup final). Both scored the goals that tied the game 3-3 in extra time. Both made their penalty kicks in the shootout. But Argentina won when France could only make one other kick. It was Messi's first World Cup trophy and pretty much made him the GOAT of world soccer.

The incredible final game capped off a record-setting World Cup. A total of 172 goals were scored in the 64 games, the most ever in a 32-team Cup. Morocco became the first team from Africa to advance to the semifinals, thrilling fans on that continent and also in the Arab world. The first-round games also saw a pack of upsets, including a win over Belgium by Morocco, that helped knock out some of the tournament favorites. Saudi Arabia surprised Argentina in both teams' first game, while Japan knocked off highly favored Germany. South Korea also beat Spain! When the dust settled, five teams from outside Europe and South America made the final 16, the most ever in a World Cup.

Then fans settled in to watch a series of incredible contests. The first two quarterfinals were classic games. Superstar **Neymar** scored for favored Brazil in extra time, but Croatia tied the game with a 117th-minute goal. Croatian goalie **Dominik Livaković** then saved a penalty kick and Brazil missed one; Croatia won 4-2 on PKs. Then the Netherlands shocked Argentina by scoring two goals, including one on a game-tying free-kick. But Argentina goalie **Emiliano Martínez** saved two shots in the penalty shootout and Argentina won 4-3. After shutting down the Spanish offense in a 0-0 tie, Morocco beat Spain in a shootout. Spain didn't even make a single penalty kick!

In the quarterfinals, England went home after losing to France in part because star striker **Harry Kane** missed a penalty kick that would have tied the game late; France won 2-1. Morocco continued its string of upsets, beating Portugal and **Cristiano Ronaldo** 1-0.

That helped set up a great pair of semifinals (page 132) and that once-in-a-lifetime final. Now fans can't wait until 2026 . . . when the World Cup will be in Mexico, Canada, and the United States!

US GAMES

US 1, WALES 1 The US team came within moments of a win in its first game. They held a strong Wales team scoreless until giving up a penalty kick in the 81st minute. **Tim Weah** scored the US goal on an assist from **Christian Pulisic**.

US 0, ENGLAND 0 Neither team scored, but the US "won" this big match against one of the world's top teams. The Americans outhustled and outshot England, earning an important point for the tie in the race to make the Round of 16.

US 1, IRAN 0 What a tense game! Pulisic (*in blue at right*) scored the game's only goal late in the first half. But he was injured and had to leave. The American defense stayed strong as Iran attacked over and over. The final minutes of extra time were dramatic, but the US held on to reach the Round of 16 for the first time since 2014.

NETHERLANDS 3, US 1 Against a very strong Dutch team, the US made some defensive mistakes but played well overall. A goal right before halftime put the team in a hole they could not escape, even after **Haji Wright** slipped in a goal in the second half. The US team could be proud of its effort on the big stage.

Defender Théo Hernandez got airborne to knock in France's first goal in the semifinal.

World Cup Semis

Argentina 3, Croatia 0

The great **Lionel Messi** had done just about everything in his career . . . except win the World Cup. He led his team one step closer with a dominating win over Croatia. Messi scored a powerful penalty kick in the first half. **Julián Álvarez** ended a 60-yard run with a flick past the Croatian keeper for goal number two. Messi then set up Álvarez for another goal after some amazing dribbling and a pinpoint pass. The loss ended Croatian legend **Luka Modrić**'s World Cup career.

France 2, Morocco 0

An acrobatic fifth-minute goal by defender **Théo Hernandez** was the first one given up by Morocco to an opponent in the World Cup. France's defense then held firm against waves of Moroccan attacks. The surprise team of the tournament gave the defending champs all they could handle. **Kylian Mbappé** set up France's second goal late in the game, dribbling through several players. His deflected shot then ended up at the feet of **Randal Kolo Muani**, who had been in the game for less than a minute. He banged it in to set off a French celebration. That set up a World Cup final between two former champions and two of the world's most famous players: Messi and Mbappé.

World Cup Final

Argentina 3, France 3
Argentina Wins PKs, 4-2

The 2022 World Cup championship game looked like a boxing match. Both teams landed big blows, trading big goals back and forth. In the end, Argentina and **Lionel Messi** saw their dream come true, while defending champ France was not able to hold on to its crown.

Argentina dominated most of the first hour of the game. Messi scored a penalty kick in the first half and helped set up a goal by **Ángel di María** in the second half. But then **Kylian Mbappé** scored two goals in less than three minutes, the second a spectacular one-time laser to the far corner of the goal. The tie led to extra time, where Messi nudged in a go-ahead goal with 11 minutes left. But the French battled back. With just three minutes left, a handball by Argentina gave Mbappé a chance to tie the game again with a PK . . . and he nailed it, giving him a hat trick.

Argentina's goalie, **Emiliano Martínez**, came up big in the penalty-kick shootout. He stopped the second French shot, and the third French shot was hit wide. Argentina made all its kicks. When **Gonzalo Montiel**'s shot hit the back of the net, it was over, and Messi and Argentina were champs. Most experts called it the best and most memorable World Cup final ever.

WORLD CUP AWARD WINNERS

GOLDEN BALL (TOP PLAYER)
LIONEL MESSI, Argentina

GOLDEN BOOT (TOP SCORER)
KYLIAN MBAPPÉ, France

GOLDEN GLOVES (TOP GOALIE)
EMILIANO MARTÍNEZ
Argentina

TOP YOUNG PLAYER
ENZO FERNÁNDEZ
Argentina

Celebration time for Argentina and Lionel Messi!

NWSL 2022

The increasing success of the National Women's Soccer League continued in 2022, as two new California-based teams made headlines with great play and packed stadiums. Angel City FC plays in Los Angeles and has a pack of celebrities among its owners, including actors Natalie Portman, Jennifer Garner, and Jessica Chastain, singer Christina Aguilera, and several former women's national team players, such as all-time great **Mia Hamm**. Led by star **Alex Morgan**, the San Diego Wave also started play in 2022 and had a terrific season, leading the league at one point before finishing third overall and becoming the first first-year team to make the playoffs. Also, in September, the two teams played at San Diego and fans there set a single-game attendance record of 32,000.

New players were emerging in 2022, too. ESPN wrote that the "2022 rookies are the best the league has ever had." **Olivia Moultrie** became the youngest goalscorer in league history. She was 16 years old when she scored for the Portland Thorns. **Savannah DeMelo** was a scoring star for Racing Louisville in her first season. The Rookie of the Year was **Naomi Girma** of San Diego, who later played several games for the US Women's National Team on defense. In fact, more than 50 NWSL stars took part in international games for more than 15 countries.

Alex Morgan

Naomi Girma (left) had a great first season, helping San Diego make the playoffs.

The NWSL did have to go through a tough time throughout the season. In late 2021, reports of abuse by coaches began to surface. The reports led to half of the league's coaches resigning or being fired. A report issued in October 2022 painted a sad picture of how athletes were treated. Players called for changes, which are continuing to be put into place. Through it all, the players stuck together, no matter what team they were on.

Back on the field, the scramble for playoff spots came down to the final weekend, with several teams having a shot at the final berths. The OL Reign also used a final-weekend 3-0 win over Orlando to clinch the NWSL Shield with the best record for the regular season. They were joined by the Portland Thorns as the top seeds.

2022 NWSL STANDINGS

PLACE/TEAM	POINTS
1. OL Reign	40
2. Portland Thorns FC	39
3. San Diego Wave FC	36
4. Houston Dash	36
5. Kansas City Current	36
6. Chicago Red Stars	33
7. North Carolina Courage	32
8. Angel City FC	29
9. Racing Louisville FC	23
10. Orlando Pride	22
11. Washington Spirit	19
12. NJ/NY Gotham FC	13

A Cup for Kerolin and the Courage

CHALLENGE CUP

The North Carolina Courage won the preseason Challenge Cup, defeating the Washington Spirit 2-1. Brazilian star **Kerolin** scored first for the Courage, but Spirit star **Ashley Hatch**, who had scored her first national-team goals a year earlier, tied the game with a well-placed shot. Both teams pressed hard in the second half, and it was only an own goal by the Spirit that put the Courage on top to stay.

2022 NWSL AWARDS

MVP
Sophia Smith
PORTLAND

ROOKIE OF THE YEAR
DEFENDER OF THE YEAR
Naomi Girma
SAN DIEGO

GOALKEEPER OF THE YEAR
Kailen Sheridan
SAN DIEGO

GOLDEN BOOT (TOP SCORER)
Ashley Hatch ▶▶▶
WASHINGTON

COACH OF THE YEAR
Casey Stoney
SAN DIEGO

NWSL Playoffs

Kristen Hamilton led KC to the finals.

Championship
Portland 2, Kansas City 0
Sophia Smith had a pretty good week. The Portland star was named the league's MVP, and several days later, she scored in the fourth minute to lead the way to the Thorns' championship victory. KC put in an own goal to double Portland's lead. The Thorns held on to earn their third NWSL title. Smith added another award, too—championship-game MVP!

Semifinals
Portland 2, San Diego 1
The Thorns spoiled the Wave's rookie-season run with a dramatic victory in front of a sold-out crowd in Portland. US Women's National Team star **Crystal Dunn** slammed in a long shot with just minutes to go in the game to give Portland a spot in the championship.

Kansas City 2, Seattle 0
Having the best record in the league didn't help the Reign in this game. **Alex Loera** and **Kristen Hamilton** scored for KC to give them their first spot in the final. Loera's goal was only in the fourth minute of the game!

A winner's smile for Sophia Smith (front)!

Fans in Charlotte welcomed their new MLS team with a record-setting crowd!

MLS 2022

Before the World Cup games started in 2022, fans in the US showed how much they like soccer by continuing to help Major League Soccer grow. More fans watched games in person than in any previous season. The numbers were up on TV, too, along with souvenir sales and even TikTok followers!

All those fans enjoyed watching some amazing soccer all summer and fall. One of the big stories came in Charlotte, North Carolina. At the first home game for the new Charlotte FC, 74,479 fans set a new MLS single-game record! The home-team fans loved the new team, the new gear, and the new excitement—but they didn't like the result. The LA Galaxy won 1-0.

MLS fans were also watching more players from around the world than ever before. Players from 82 different countries were on MLS rosters when the season started. The US was home to most, while Canada was second, followed by Argentina.

LAFC got off to the hottest start in the league. They lost only one of their first 10 games. In the summer, they had a seven-game winning streak, too! Later in the season, they showed how much they were focused on a title by adding international superstars **Giorgio Chiellini** from Italy and **Gareth Bale** from Wales. Fans in Texas were thrilled by the success of Austin FC. In only its second season, it had one of the Western Conference's best records.

On the East Coast, Philadelphia was putting together a great season as well, led by star goalie **Andre Blake**. While LAFC was hot early, Philly was strong late, including an 11–2 run heading into the season's final weeks. Both New York teams—NYCFC and the Red Bulls—were also strong, finishing in the top four.

The final Sunday saw four teams clinch playoff spots. Meanwhile, Seattle missed out on the playoffs for the first time since 2009, ending one of the longest postseason appearance streaks in major North American men's sports. LAFC did indeed wind up with the best record, earning the Supporters' Shield for the second time in four seasons.

2022 MLS AWARDS

MVP
Hany Mukhtar
NASHVILLE

NEWCOMER OF THE YEAR
Thiago Almada
ATLANTA

COMEBACK PLAYER OF THE YEAR
Gonzalo Higuaín
MIAMI

DEFENDER OF THE YEAR
Jakob Glesnes
PHILADELPHIA

GOALKEEPER OF THE YEAR
Andre Blake
PHILADELPHIA

COACH OF THE YEAR
Jim Curtin
PHILADELPHIA

Of course, by now, you've seen that **Lionel Messi** joined Inter Miami in the summer of 2023. Adding the world's biggest superstar is one of the biggest things ever to happen to MLS.

Philly's Andre Blake set a record by earning his third Goalkeeper of the Year honor.

MLS Conference Finals

Julián Carranza

LAFC 3, AUSTIN 0

The team with the season's best record put aside a playoff jinx for a big win. A header by **Cristian Arango** started the scoring as LAFC put a ton of pressure on the Austin defense in the first half. Austin put in an own goal in the second half, and **Kwadwo "Mahala" Opoku** cemented the LAFC win with a late goal. Their win meant that LAFC would host the MLS Cup for the first time.

PHILADELPHIA 3, NYCFC 1

The Union got revenge for a 2021 conference-final loss, coming back from a goal down to beat the defending MLS champs. A big save by goalie **Andre Blake** kept NYC from doubling their lead, and then the Philly offense poured in three second-half goals to win the conference title. **Julián Carranza** and **Dániel Gazdag** scored close together to capture the lead. A goal near the end by **Cory Burke** made up the final score. Like LAFC, Philly had the best record in its conference, so the two top teams would meet in the final.

John McCarthy was the surprise hero for LAFC, stopping two PKs to seal the title.

MLS Cup 2022

LAFC 3, Philadelphia 3
LAFC Wins PKs, 3-0

This was an instant classic, with fans and experts calling it the best MLS game ever played in the league's 27 seasons. It featured the top two teams, it included the Hollywood style of LAFC, and it took every second of action to decide a winner. LAFC dominated early play and took a 2-1 lead late in regular time on a header by **Jesús Murillo**. But Philly tied it two minutes later with **Jack Elliott**'s header. In overtime, LAFC goalie **Maxime Crépeau** had to come way out of his box to slide-tackle and foul a Philly player. The goalie was ejected with a red card due to the foul . . . and he also suffered a broken leg! Against backup goalie **John McCarthy**, Elliott snuck in a goal in extra time. But with just a minute left, LAFC's international superstar **Gareth Bale** rose above the crowd to smash in a shocking, game-tying goal. Wow! McCarthy then came up huge in the shootout, stopping two PKs, while LAFC made three straight. It was the first MLS Cup win for LAFC, the league's top-winning team over the past five seasons.

Champions League 2023

The UEFA Champions League is probably the second-most-watched soccer tournament after the World Cup. Dozens of top European teams go through a tournament that takes months to play. But only one team gets to end up a winner! (Note: The semifinals are a two-game series; the winner is decided by total goals.)

MEN'S

SEMIFINALS:

Manchester City 5, Real Madrid 1

City was on its way to being the 2023 Premier League champ, while Madrid was the defending Champions League winner. Fans expected a tight match, and they got it in the first leg, as City's **Kevin de Bruyne** had to make a long shot to earn a 1-1 tie. However, in the second leg, City dominated. **Bernardo Silva** scored twice on City's way to a 4-0 win.

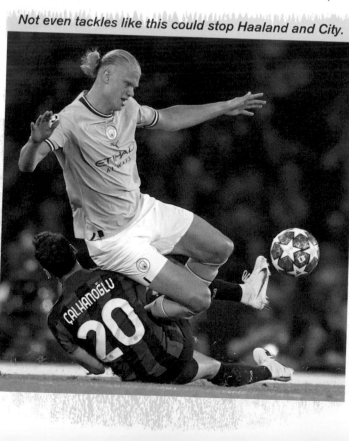

Not even tackles like this could stop Haaland and City.

Inter Milan 3, AC Milan 0

A pair of Italian teams from the same city were fighting for the other spot in the final. Both teams share the same stadium, too! Inter got two goals in the first 11 minutes of the first game, and AC never threatened, losing the second game 1-0.

FINAL

Manchester City 1, Inter Milan 0

Manchester City did it. For the first time since 1999, a Premier League team completed the famous "treble" (that's British for triple!). City won the Premier League, the FA Cup, and, thanks to a goal by **Rodri**, this year's Champions League. Inter made City work and didn't allow super-scorer **Erling Haaland** much room. City's goal came on a second-half mistake by the Inter defense that left Rodri free. His right-footed shot was the only goal City needed.

Pauline Bremer slid this goal home to put Wolfsburg into the final.

WOMEN'S

The women's European championship had a different look as the semifinals began. For one of the few times in the past decade, France's Olympique Lyonnais did not make the final four. Chelsea had knocked out the eight-time champ in penalties in the quarterfinal. Who would be the new champ for 2023? (Note: The semifinals are a two-game series; the winner is decided by total goals.)

SEMIFINALS:
Barcelona 2, Chelsea 1
Caroline Graham Hansen scored in both legs of this semifinal to put Barcelona into the championship game. Chelsea tied the second game 1-1 but could not find another goal against a tough Barca defense.

They had to settle for winning the Women's Super League (page 144).

Wolfsburg 5, Arsenal 4
A shocking goal with just one minute to play in extra time of the second game sent Wolfsburg to the final. The two teams had tied the first leg 2-2 and were tied 2-2 again in the second leg. They played nearly 30 minutes of extra time before **Pauline Bremer** scored the winner from short range.

FINAL
Barcelona 3, Wolfsburg 2
Barcelona looked like it was in trouble. Wolfsburg led 2-0 at halftime on goals from **Ewa Pajor** and **Alexandra Popp**. Everything changed when **Patricia Guijarro** scored two goals for Barcelona in five minutes! In the 70th minute, Barcelona's **Fridolina Rolfö** banged in the winner.

2022–23 Premier League

Haaland broke the single-season goals record.

have new striker **Erling Haaland**, however. The big Norwegian dominated just about every game he was in. He set a new EPL record with 36 goals, and another with his 52 goals in all the team's games (including cups and other tournaments). At one point, he had hat tricks in three straight games! Still, his team began 2023 in second place and lost to last-place Southampton in January. But soon after that, they went on an 11-match winning streak, which included defeating Arsenal. Arsenal began to fade just as City romped, and the men in light blue won their fourth straight Premier League title. No surprise: Haaland was named the Premier League Player of the Year and Luton Town earned a spot in next year's Premier League for the first time in 31 years!

For quite a while, it looked like the English Premier League would have a new champion. Arsenal got off to a hot start while three-time defending champ Manchester City struggled a bit. City did

Women's Super League

Women's soccer in England has its own dominating team: Chelsea. The club from London became the first team in WSL history to win a fourth straight championship. It was a closer battle than most years, and Chelsea had to beat Reading 3-0 on the final day to clinch the trophy. Australian star **Sam Kerr** was the team's top scorer and was named the WSL Player of the Year.

Key Leagues: 2022-23

Spain

Barcelona had a double celebration in 2023, as both its men's and women's teams won their national championships. The men's team won for the first time since 2019, letting its fans breathe a sigh of relief. After all, they had won 26 titles in the past, second most all-time. Meanwhile, Barca's women's team continued its great run, winning its fourth championship in a row. How good were they? They won 26 of 26 games!

Germany

Bayern Munich has dominated Germany's Bundesliga, winning ten titles in a row. That streak was in doubt until the final minutes of the final weekend. A win by Borussia Dortmund would make them champions and disappoint Bayern. However, Dortmund could manage only a tie, and Munich won its game, earning its 11th straight title. The Bayern women's team didn't have as much trouble, winning 11-1 in its final game to take home the season trophy.

Lionel Messi

France

Led by megastars **Lionel Messi** and **Kylian Mbappé**, Paris Saint-Germain won the Ligue 1 title in France. The defending champs made it two in a row and became the first team to win the national title 11 times. Player of the year **Delphine Cascarino** led Olympique Lyonnais to its 16th women's championship. Lyon has been so dominant that it has missed finishing on top only once since 2007! The team lost just one game in the 2022-23 season.

Mexico

Liga MX crowns champs from two tournaments, one at the beginning of the season (Apertura) and one at the end (Clausura). In 2022, Pachuca won the first, while in 2023, Tigres came from behind to win the second. The women's Liga MX champion came down to a battle between América and Pachuca, with América coming out on top 4-2.

NASCAR

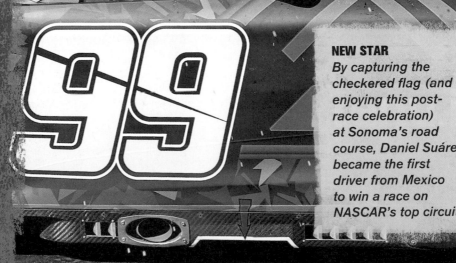

NEW STAR
By capturing the checkered flag (and enjoying this post-race celebration) at Sonoma's road course, Daniel Suárez became the first driver from Mexico to win a race on NASCAR's top circuit.

NASCAR Season 2022

NASCAR debuted the new Next Gen car design for the 2022 racing season. The goal was to even the playing field between rich teams and not-so-rich teams. The plan worked . . . almost too well! There were a record-tying 19 different winners throughout the whole season, including five drivers who won their first race. In the end, though, it was the oldest playoff driver who carried home the final checkered flag.

The season started with Austin Cindric as the surprise winner of the Daytona 500. Over the course of the following few weeks, some familiar names won races to earn playoff spots, including Kyle Larson, Alex Bowman, and Denny Hamlin. Rising stars Chase Briscoe and Ross Chastain earned their spots in the playoff with their first NASCAR victories.

One of the midseason highlights was watching NBA legend Michael Jordan win a NASCAR race! Well, okay, the Hall of Famer didn't actually drive, but he does co-own the car! Jordan's racing team driver Kurt Busch sped past the field to win the race at Kansas in May. Busch's car even sported No. 45, one of the uniform numbers Jordan wore in his fantastic career.

A back-and-forth battle led to a final-lap sprint at the June race in Illinois. When the dust cleared, Joey Logano had earned his second win of the year. He dueled with Kyle Busch after earlier crashes had tightened up the field.

At Sonoma, Daniel Suárez won and made history as the first driver from Mexico to win a NASCAR Cup Series race. The road course surprises continued as the season went on. Chastain won at the Circuit of the Americas in Texas, while Tyler Reddick captured his first checkered flag when he won at Elkhart Lake in Wisconsin.

How do you win . . . and lose? Hamlin roared across the finish line at the race in Pennsylvania in July. He was followed by Kyle Busch. But after the race, an inspection showed that both cars had parts that were not approved by NASCAR. For the first time since 1960, a race winner was disqualified. Chase Elliott was named the winner, even though he had finished third!

In August at Michigan, veteran Kevin Harvick broke a 65-race losing streak, earning a playoff spot with three weeks to go.

The final playoff spot fell to Austin Dillon on the final day as rain fell, too! Dillon was in the lead when weather paused the race at Daytona. After a three-hour delay, Dillon was able to race to the checkered flag and earn a playoff spot. Read on to see who wound up in first place!

First-Time Winners

Look for these young drivers to make more marks on the NASCAR circuit in the years to come. They all won their first race in 2022.

Austin Cindric (Daytona)

Chase Briscoe (Phoenix)

Ross Chastain (Texas)

Daniel Suárez (Sonoma)

Tyler Reddick (Road America)

Chris Buescher (front left) kept the wild start of the Chase for the Cup going in Bristol.

2022 CHASE FOR THE CUP!

ROUND ONE

DARLINGTON: The Chase for the Cup playoffs got off to a wild start! Almost all the points leaders ran into trouble (or walls . . . or each other!). Kevin Harvick's car even caught on fire (he was okay)! The race winner was Erik Jones, who is not even in the playoffs! No racer moved automatically into the next round. The points race was scrambled, with No. 1 Chase Elliott falling all the way to ninth!

KANSAS: For the second week in a row, a non-playoff driver won the race. Bubba Wallace cruised to his second career victory ahead of Denny Hamlin. With just one race left in the first section of the playoffs, the battle to move on remained tight. Several former champions were at risk of being left behind!

BRISTOL: What, again? For the third time in a row this year (and first time ever in the playoffs), a non-playoff driver won this race! Chris Buescher became the 19th different winner in 2022. When the points were totaled after the race, four drivers were eliminated from the playoffs, including two former champs.

OUT: Kyle Busch, Austin Dillon, Kevin Harvick, Tyler Reddick

ROUND TWO

TEXAS: One guess who won here: That's right—a non-playoff driver! In a race that included a record 36 lead changes, Tyler Reddick ended up in first on a wild day that also included an hourlong rain delay! Joey Logano moved into first place in the playoff points by finishing second.

TALLADEGA: Finally! Elliott became the first playoff driver to win one of the 2022 Playoff races! He took advantage of a late restart to zoom from fifth to first and then held off a charging Ryan Blaney. Elliott moved on to the next round automatically, while the rest of the playoff racers had one more race to fight for the other seven spots.

CHARLOTTE: Christopher Bell had to win this race or he'd be out of the playoffs. On the "roval," a combined oval and road track, the former Xfinity Series driver came through with a checkered flag and booked a ticket to the Round of Eight.

OUT: Alex Bowman, Austin Cindric, Kyle Larson, Daniel Suárez

ROUND OF EIGHT

LAS VEGAS: A bold late move to put on fresh tires proved to be the right one for Logano. He roared to the front of the race and never looked back. His victory made him the first driver to clinch a spot in the championship, coming up in Phoenix.

MIAMI: Though he couldn't be in the championship, Kyle Larson still knew how to win. He held off Ross Chastain to win the season's next-to-last race. Other playoff drivers piled up points behind him, setting up a showdown in West Virginia. In that race at Martinsville, seven drivers would battle for the three spots left in the championship.

MARTINSVILLE: What a finish! Bell won the race to clinch a spot in the championship. But Chastain was the real story. On the final part of the last lap, he slammed his car into the curving wall and sped up, hugging the wall around the final turn and increasing speed to pass several cars. His metal-scraping run gave him enough points to join Bell, Logano, and Elliott in the race for the Cup.

Chase Elliott's win at Talladega broke a streak of wins by non-playoff drivers.

Other NASCAR Champs

TRUCK SERIES

On the final weekend of the 2022 season, three champions were crowned. The first came in the Camping World Truck Series. **Zane Smith** had finished second twice but broke through on the final laps this year to win his first series title. The race ended in an overtime sprint after a late crash brought out the yellow caution flag. Smith held off **Ben Rhodes** and **Chandler Smith** to grab the checkered flag and the trophy.

Zane Smith put on a tire-smoking victory celebration!

XFINITY SERIES

While the Cup race was not that close, this series ended with a race-long battle among three drivers. In the end, **Ty Gibbs** led the most laps and was in first place at the end, capturing his first Xfinity Series championship. **Noah Gragson** was among the drivers making it close, steadily moving toward Gibbs's lead . . . but they couldn't catch him. Ty is the grandson of team owner **Joe Gibbs**. Sadly, Ty's dad—and Joe's son—**Coy Gibbs**, died unexpectedly the night of Ty's win.

Ty Gibbs's win soon turned to sadness.

2022 Championship Race

Phoenix

This race was mostly over from the start, as polesitter Joey Logano roared into the lead and almost never gave it up. Holding off the three other playoff finalists, as well as the rest of the field, the veteran driver earned his second NASCAR championship—the first came in 2018. His team owner, the legendary Roger Penske, completed a rare double; this NASCAR win matched Penske's team's win in IndyCar (page 154) as well. Ross Chastain finished third, the closest of the four playoff racers to Logano, who celebrated with his four-year-old Hudson waving the flag as his dad waved to the crowd.

Logano earned the huge series Cup.

Joey Logano had most of the field in his rearview mirror throughout the final race.

OTHER MOTOR SPORTS

THE CAR OF THE CHAMPION
Max Verstappen set a single-season victory record while cruising to his second straight Formula 1 season championship. The Dutch driver clinched the title with four races left!

Formula 1 2022

After 2021 provided fans with the most exciting, down-to-the-last-lap finish in recent Formula 1 history, 2022 was pretty much the opposite. In 2021, **Max Verstappen** won his first title on the last lap of the last race. He made it much easier in 2022, clinching the championship with four races remaining! He also won 15 races, breaking the record of 13 set by the great **Michael Schumacher** in 2004.

As the 2022 schedule began, with everyone watching Verstappen's Red Bull versus **Lewis Hamilton**'s Mercedes, Ferrari's **Charles Leclerc** won two of the season's first five races. Verstappen won the other three. However, he did not even finish the two races Leclerc won! Verstappen's biggest early win was in Miami, when he overtook polesitter Leclerc and held on for the win. It was the first Grand Prix race held in Miami and was one of three held in North America in 2022.

Verstappen kept it rolling with a win in Azerbaijan. Even as Verstappen extended his lead, other drivers climbed the standings. In Great Britain, **Carlos Sainz Jr.** won his first career F1 race. The race had a scary beginning. As the cars roared away from the start line, **Zhou Guanyu** ran into other cars, and then his car started rolling over and over. It slid upside down into tire barriers and then flipped over! Amazingly, he was unhurt, but the race was stopped while the track was cleared.

In the French Grand Prix, Leclerc had a great chance to gain a few points on Verstappen. But in front of his home-country fans, the French driver made a mistake and crashed his car, knocking him out of the race. Verstappen took advantage and roared to his seventh win of the season, extending his lead to 63 points.

In the Netherlands, Verstappen added another big milestone to his dominant season. He won the Dutch Grand Prix, a career first for him, for his fourth straight win. Doing it in front of his home-country fans made that win even sweeter. With a win in Italy—the first time he had finished on the podium in that famous race—Verstappen had pretty much locked up the season title.

A seventh-place finish in Singapore slowed down Verstappen's drive to the top. But he got to cheer for his teammate, **Sergio Pérez**, who won his second race.

The Dutch driver made it official in Japan, with a twist. Rain poured on the track for most of this race, causing several stoppages. Eventually, the race was called with 24 laps left, but enough laps had been run for it to be official. It took a while for the points to be counted up, so Verstappen didn't know he had clinched the title until he was doing a post-match interview!

FINAL F1 2022 STANDINGS

PLACE, DRIVER, COUNTRY	POINTS
1. **Max Verstappen**, USA	454
2. **Charles Leclerc**, France	308
3. **Sergio Pérez**, Mexico	305
4. **George Russell**, Great Britain	275
5. **Carlos Sainz Jr.**, Spain	246

2022 IndyCar

Who had the "power" to win the 2022 IndyCar championship? It was a battle among several racers, but in the end, one had the "will" to win.

The 2022 IndyCar season began by welcoming **Jimmie Johnson**, a seven-time NASCAR champ, as a regular series driver. Though Johnson was used to going very fast, he took a while to adjust to the racing style of the twisting, turning IndyCar tracks. At Long Beach in the season's third race, he broke his hand in a crash during practice. Johnson raced anyway . . . and crashed again! **Josef Newgarden** roared ahead of polesitter **Colton Herta** to win his second race in a row after getting the checkered flag in Texas. Herta got his revenge two weeks later with a win on the Indy road course. Meanwhile, **Will Power** was the steadiest driver in the early going, with five straight top-five finishes, to put him in first place in the standings.

At Road America in June, Newgarden won his third race of the season and inched closer to the top of the standings.

But he was behind Sweden's **Marcus Ericsson**, who became the second driver from that country to win the famous Indianapolis 500 at the end of May.

Power finally got his first win in Detroit. The Australian star kept **Alexander Rossi** from passing him on the final lap. It was the final race at Detroit's Belle Isle racetrack.

At Mid-Ohio, **Scott McLaughlin** won the second race of his career, but this one was special. This driver is from New Zealand, and because of COVID, he had not seen his parents in almost three years. But they finally made it to the US in time to see their son roar to victory.

Will Power hoists the trophy after winning the IndyCar title.

INDY 500 '23

More than 230,000 people packed the Indianapolis Speedway for the 107th edition of the most famous auto race in America. And for the first time since 2016, an American–**Josef Newgarden**–drove under the checkered flag! Newgarden and the field had to wait through three red flags caused by crashes. The final stoppage left just one lap left. On the restart, Newgarden slingshotted his way past 2022 Indy 500 champ **Marcus Ericsson** for his first-ever Indy 500 win in his 12th try here. To celebrate? A traditional bottle of Indiana milk!

A double-race weekend at Iowa saw one polesitter and a pair of winners—neither from the pole! Power qualified first in both races, but he finished behind Newgarden in the first race and **Pato O'Ward** in the second. With four races to go, Power took over the points lead by finishing third at Indianapolis. With a win the following week in Nashville, veteran driver **Scott Dixon** passed the great **Mario Andretti** for second-most checkered flags of all time. At Illinois, Power broke Andretti's record for most pole positions.

At Portland, with a week to go in the season, McLaughlin won, finishing ahead of Power, but Power still held on to a 20-point lead. With one race to go, it all came down to Laguna Seca in California.

In that final race, Power needed to finish third to earn enough points to hold on to the title. Though he was pushed throughout the race by former champ **Álex Palou** and Penske Motorsports teammate Josef Newgarden, Power did the job. As he passed the finish line, he was in third for the day and first for the year. It was his first IndyCar title since 2014.

FINAL INDYCAR STANDINGS

PLACE, DRIVER, COUNTRY	POINTS
1. **Will Power**, Australia	560
2. **Josef Newgarden**, USA	544
3. **Scott Dixon**, New Zealand	521
4. **Scott McLaughlin**, New Zealand	510
5. **Álex Palou**, Spain	510

Drag Racing

TOP FUEL: At the Finals, **Brittany Force** continued her season-long domination, piling up enough points in qualifying to clinch her second season championship. She also won the top spot in 2017. Force had six of the top 10 fastest runs of the season and won five events in drag racing's fastest series.

FUNNY CAR: One of the closest season titles in NHRA history came down to the final race of this series. **Ron Capps** had climbed from 61 points behind to just three points ahead. He had to finish the final race without any penalties . . . and he did! Capps steered his massive machine to a clean final run to win the season championship. It was his second title in a row and third all-time.

PRO STOCK: **Erica Enders** knew she would make history, it was just a matter of when. She won event after event, ending up with an amazing 10 victories. Her runaway championship was the fifth of her career, making her the first woman to reach that many Pro Stock season titles and only the fifth driver ever.

PRO STOCK: Motorcycle: **Matt Smith** joined a small club, too, when he won his sixth career season championship, clinching it with a qualifying race in the final event of 2022. Smith became only the third racer ever with that many motorcycle drag-racing titles. He won his first back in 2007, and his 2022 win was also his third in a row.

Erica Enders made history in Pro Stock.

Motorcycle Racing

SUPERCROSS

The action in the muddy, indoor Supercross series was wilder than usual. Several top contenders crashed more than usual, and a new winner emerged. **Chase Sexton** had three of his six 2023 450cc race victories to finish with a late-season kick that pushed him ahead of last year's champ, **Eli Tomac**, on points. Sexton also had seven other top-three finishes for a consistently solid season. A pair of brothers made brotherly history in the 250cc class. **Jett Lawrence** won the West 250cc with six race wins of his own, while his brother **Hunter Lawrence** was the East 250cc overall winner. All three champion riders rode for the Honda team, a rare "triple crown" for a motorcycle maker.

Chase Sexton

Francesco Bagnaia

MOTO GP

How do you finish ninth and become the world champion? By piling up so many points by the last race, that ninth is good enough! That's how **Francesco Bagnaia** won the 2022 MotoGP championship. Incredibly, Bagnaia was all the way in sixth place with just eight races left, but roared through the field to finish on top for the first time in his career. It was especially sweet, because Bagnaia, who is from Italy, rides for Italian bike maker Ducati, and this was that sponsor's first title since 2007! MotoGP is somewhat like the Formula 1 of motorcycle racing. Around since 1949, the sport features riders speeding down long straights and around hairpin turns—often nearly touching the ground with their knees!

GOLF

NICE VIEW!
Allisen Corpuz tees off on the seventh hole at majestic Pebble Beach during the final round of the 2023 US Women's Open. Corpuz won her first LPGA title at the first women's major held at the famous seaside course. *(See page 163.)*

Golf 2022

The 2022 men's golf season was confusing, to say the least. Many of the biggest stars in the world left the PGA Tour to join LIV Golf (LIV is pronounced like the verb "live," as in "live and breathe"). Fans were not sure where to see their favorites. The split turned player against player off the course. (See page 164.) There were still lots of highlights on the course, away from the confusion.

PRESIDENTS CUP

The US Team beat the International Team 17.5-12.5 at the Quail Hollow Club in Charlotte, North Carolina, to win the Cup for the ninth time in a row. The US won four of the five matches on the opening day of the competition, and the outcome was never in doubt. **Jordan Spieth** led the way by winning all five of the matches in which he competed. **Max Homa** won all four of his, and **Justin Thomas** added four wins in five matches.

PGA NOTES

✳ **Tony Finau** is the first player of Tongan and Samoan descent to play on the PGA Tour. He had a great run in the summer of 2022. First, he won the 3M Open in Blaine, Minn. The next week, he won the Rocket Mortgage Classic in Detroit to become the PGA's first back-to-back winner since 2019. He finished the season in ninth place in the FedEx Cup standings.

✳ The winner of the 2022 FedEx Cup—and of the $18 million check that comes with it—was **Rory McIlroy**. With a score of 66, the world's No. 1–ranked player overtook **Scottie Scheffler**, the PGA Tour's Player of the Year, in the final round of the season-ending Tour Championship in Atlanta.

LPGA STARS

✳ **Ashleigh Buhai**'s first LPGA Tour victory was a big one. The South African won the final women's major of 2022 when she beat South Korea's **In Gee Chun** in a playoff at the Women's British Open in Muirfield, Scotland.

✳ **Lydia Ko** of New Zealand won the season-ending Tour Championship in Naples, Florida. Ko's victory made her the LPGA Tour's Player of the Year, which is based on points. She also won the Vare Trophy for the lowest-scoring average of the season. And, of course, she got $2 million for winning the tournament.

Finau celebrates a win in Detroit.

Around the Links: 2023

First-time champ Rose Zhang

Welcome to the Pros!

Rose Zhang didn't exactly come out of nowhere. In 2020, she won the US Women's Amateur. In 2022 and 2023 at Stanford, she was the first women's two-time NCAA champion. Still, that was only a warm-up to her first pro event. Less than two weeks after her 20th birthday, the California-born Zhang rolled in a par putt on the second playoff hole to win the Mizuho Americas Open in New Jersey.

Team Thailand

In 2023, for the first time in five years, the LPGA schedule included a team match play event. The International Crown was played at Harding Park in San Francisco in May. Led by **Atthaya Thitikul**, the Thailand team won. Thitikul won all five of her matches for the week, and her team swept Australia 3-0 in the final. Team USA beat Sweden to take third place.

O, Canada!

For the first time in 69 years, a Canadian man won the Canadian Open. **Nick Taylor**, who was born in Winnipeg, did it in 2023 in amazing fashion. He rolled in a 72-foot putt for an eagle

62 The US Open record score posted by both **Rickie Fowler** and **Xander Schauffele** in the first round in Los Angeles in June 2023. The old record was 63. Fowler and Schauffele were near the top throughout the tournament, but **Wyndham Clark** won it.

Crowns and medals for the champion Team Thailand, led by Atthaya Thitikul (right)

on the fifth extra hole to beat England's **Tommy Fleetwood**. Taylor had shot red-hot rounds of 63 and 66 on the weekend to make it into the playoff. He was the first Canadian citizen to win the men's Canadian Open since 1954, and the first player born In Canada to win since 1914.

Canadian Open winner Nick Taylor

Finish With a Flourish

Michelle Wie West played her final round of pro golf at the US Women's Open in July 2023. The 33-year-old Wie, who was born in Hawaii, was one of the biggest names in women's golf when she turned pro at 16 in 2005. She went on to win five times on the LPGA Tour, including the US Women's Open in 2014. Wie didn't do well at the 2023 tournament, missing the cut. But she closed her career in style, curling in a 31-foot putt on the famed 18th hole at Pebble Beach.

2023 Men's Majors

Clark blasted to his first major win.

MEN'S MAJOR CHAMPIONS 2023

MASTERS	**Jon Rahm**
PGA CHAMPIONSHIP	**Brooks Koepka**
US OPEN	**Wyndham Clark**
BRITISH OPEN	**Brian Harman**

career win in the PGA Championship. The only players ever with more are golf legends **Walter Hagen** (five), **Jack Nicklaus** (five), and **Tiger Woods** (four).

Plot Twist

Some of the biggest stars in golf fought down to the wire at the 2023 US Open: **Rory McIlroy**, **Scottie Scheffler**, **Cameron Smith**, and **Rickie Fowler**, to name a few. But in the end, it was the surprising **Wyndham Clark** who took the trophy. Ranked No. 158, Clark had never finished higher than 75th in a major championship before. On the other hand, McIlroy, Scheffler, and Smith were ranked one-two-three in the first rankings of 2023.

British Open

Brian Harman shows you don't have to be big and strong to win at golf. He's only 5 feet, 7 inches, and he was only No. 159 in driving distance. At the 2023 British Open, though, he was accurate and putted like a dream. He never needed three putts on any green and made 59 of 60 putts of less than 15 feet. That led to a six-stroke win!

Masterful

Spain's **Jon Rahm** entered the final round of the Masters two shots behind leader **Brooks Koepka**. Rahm caught Koepka by the third hole, then passed him for good on the sixth hole. Rahm finished with a 69 to become the first European golfer to win both the Masters and the US Open.

Five for Brooks

After Koepka fell short at the 2023 Masters, he made sure he didn't let the next men's major get away. He won his fifth career major at the PGA Championship in May. The victory marked Koepka's third

2023 Women's Majors

Splashdown

For more than 30 years, the winner of the Chevron Championship jumped into the pond next to the 18th green at the course in Rancho Mirage, California. But when the tournament moved to The Woodlands, Texas, in 2023, would the winner jump? After all, people had seen snakes and alligators in that water! **Lilia Vu** made the plunge. After winning her first major with a birdie putt on the final hole, she took the leap

WOMEN'S MAJOR CHAMPIONS 2023	
CHEVRON CHAMPIONSHIP	**Lilia Vu**
WOMEN'S PGA CHAMPIONSHIP	**Ruoning Yin**
US WOMEN'S OPEN	**Allisen Corpuz**
EVIAN CHAMPIONSHIP	**Céline Boutier**
WOMEN'S BRITISH OPEN	**Lilia Vu**

into the murky water. Tournament organizers also had installed gator nets . . . just in case!

Vu (left) continued the splash tradition.

China Champ

Ruoning Yin won the women's second major of 2023, the Women's PGA Championship in June. Yin became just the second major winner from China.

Dream Big

Pebble Beach was the star in the lead up to the 78th US Women's Open in July 2023. The famous California course was hosting its first women's major. With a final-round 69, American golfer **Allisen Corpuz** took command. Throughout the final round, Corpuz's calm attitude never changed. When she finally hit her last putt, she put on a big smile, followed by tears of joy. "This is a dream come true," she said.

Finally . . . French!

The Evian Championship in France has been around since 1994, but had never had a French winner. The wait ended when **Céline Boutier** shot four rounds in the 60s and won by six strokes.

LIV Golf Report

Golf fans want to see booming drives and long, winding putts drop into the cup—not lawyers battling it out in a courtroom or players arguing on Twitter. It was a tough year for golfers and golf fans due to the split between the PGA Tour and the new LIV Golf.

UPDATE:
ALL IN THE FAMILY

Even before the first LIV golf event was held in June 2022, a war of words raged between the new league and the PGA Tour. There were lawsuits and more lawsuits. Suddenly, in June 2023, the two sides agreed to merge. They would become one big, happy family–maybe. What exactly will the new deal mean for golf? The details are still being worked out, but the rivalry between the two seems to be over. One big issue is that the money for the team-up comes from Saudi Arabia. Many feel that that country does not treat its people well or fairly. Will bad feelings remain? Will Americans watch the new golf tour sponsored by the Saudis? Keep an eye on the fairways for news!

LIV Golf's Brooks Koepka

54

That's what the Roman numerals LIV stand for. (Super Bowl LIV, for instance, was the 54th Super Bowl.) It's also the number of holes in a LIV Golf tournament. And it represents a "perfect score" on a par-72 golf course, if a player were to birdie every hole.

LIV 2022

The first LIV Golf season featured eight tournaments in 2022. They were played in cities all around the world, including London, Boston, Chicago, and Bangkok. **Dustin Johnson** (left), the No. 1–ranked player in the world for a total of 130 weeks during his career, was the runaway champion. His team, the 4Aces, won the season-ending team title, as well as the season-long team points title. The other 4Aces included **Talor Gooch**, **Pat Perez**, and **Patrick Reed**.

LIV 2023

Early in the season, **Brooks Koepka** won at Orlando to become LIV Golf's first two-time winner. (Koepka had won in Saudi Arabia in 2022.) But then Gooch won three times in a five-tournament stretch to become the first three-time victor. At midseason, Gooch, now playing for RangeGoats, had a slight lead over **Cameron Smith** of Ripper in the individual points race. But the 4Aces, with **Peter Uihlein** taking Gooch's spot on that team, still led the team standings.

TENNIS

ON TOP OF THE WORLD
Carlos Alcaraz celebrates after winning match point at Wimbledon in the summer of 2023. Alcaraz defeated Novak Djokovic in the final to become the No. 1–ranked player in men's tennis. (See page 169.)

Tennis 2022

It had to happen sometime: After nearly two decades of dominating men's tennis, the Big Three—**Roger Federer**, **Rafael Nadal**, and **Novak Djokovic**—finally started to break up in 2022. The silver lining: A new star emerged in Spain's **Carlos Alcaraz**.

Rivals and Friends

Federer was the first of the Big Three to retire. The Swiss star, who was the first men's player to win 20 Grand Slam singles titles, was never the same after suffering a knee injury early in 2020. He played his last match at Laver Cup in September 2022, teaming with Spain's Nadal for Team Europe against Americans **Jack Sock** and **Frances Tiafoe** of Team World. Federer and Nadal lost in a tight, third-set tiebreaker, but the real story was the emotional tribute paid to Federer. The man who took Federer's retirement the hardest might have been Nadal. The two all-time greats squared off 40 times in singles matches over the years, including 24 times in event finals.

Laver Cup

The Laver Cup, named for Australian tennis legend **Rod Laver**, is a three-day team competition featuring men's players from Europe against the rest of the world. Each day comprises three singles matches and one doubles match. Teams get one point for winning a match on the first day, two for winning on the second day, and three for winning on the third day. The first side to 13 points wins the competition.

In 2022, Team World, captained by American tennis great **John McEnroe**,

Świątek captured the 2022 US Open.

beat Team Europe, captained by former Swedish star **Björn Borg** 13–8 at the O2 Arena in London.

US Open

It looked as if the 2022 US Open might be known more for who wasn't there—Federer was injured and Djokovic withdrew because of the US vaccination requirements—than who was. But then great play on both the men's and women's sides grabbed the spotlight in Flushing, New York, in late August and early September.

Poland's **Iga Świątek** won the women's final in straight sets over Tunisia's **Ons Jabeur**. Świątek, who won the French Open earlier in the year, became the first woman in six years to win more than one Grand Slam singles title in a given season. The next day, Spain's Alcaraz also won his second Grand Slam of the year. He won the final over **Casper Ruud** of Norway.

Women's 2023 Grand Slams

With No. 1–ranked Ash Barty retiring in March of 2022 and former longtime No. 1 Serena Williams following suit six months later, women's tennis entered the 2023 Grand Slam season in search of a new top star. Iga Świątek may have filled the void when she won her fourth major title before her 23rd birthday.

Open Season

Without home country hero Barty, the Australian Open in January was up for grabs. Sure enough, upsets were all over Down Under. Only two of the top 16 seeds made it as far as the quarterfinals, and only one of those—No. 5 Aryna Sabalenka of Belarus—made it to the semis. Sabalenka avoided the upset bug and beat 22nd-seeded Elena Rybakina of Kazakhstan in the final. Sabalenka didn't drop a set the entire tournament until losing the opener of the final.

2023 WOMEN'S GRAND SLAMS

AUSTRALIAN OPEN	**Aryna Sabalenka**
FRENCH OPEN	**Iga Świątek**
WIMBLEDON	**Markéta Vondroušová**
US OPEN	**Coco Gauff**

She's No. 1

On the verge of losing a Grand Slam final for the first time, Świątek suddenly performed like the No. 1–ranked player she was, taking the final three games against unseeded Karolína Muchová of Czechia to win the French Open for the third time. The score in the deciding set was 6-4.

The victory put Świątek in some elite company. She joined Monica Seles and Naomi Osaka as the only women since 1968 to win each of the first four times they reached a Grand Slam final.

Big Jump

Markéta Vondroušová of Czechia was the surprise winner of the women's singles title at Wimbledon. How big a surprise? Until Vondroušová beat Ons Jabeur in straight sets in the final, no unseeded woman had ever won the tournament. With the win, she leaped from No. 42 in the world rankings to No. 10.

Wimbledon winner Vondroušová.

Men's 2023 Grand Slams

Novak Djokovic made history during the men's Grand Slam season in 2023. He set a new career record for most Slam titles. But in the end, it was **Carlos Alcaraz** who showed that the men's tennis torch has passed to a new generation.

A Good Start

Djokovic won the Australian Open in January. He beat **Stefanos Tsitsipas** of Greece in straight sets in the final. The win marked Djokovic's 22nd career Grand Slam singles title, tying **Rafael Nadal** for the most ever. It was also Djokovic's 10th victory at the Australian Open, which was also a record. Nadal, the defending champion, suffered an upset loss in the second round.

Historic Win

In June, it was strange to see a French Open final without Nadal in it. The Spanish superstar was an expert on the tournament's red-clay courts. He had won the event a record 14 times from 2005 through 2022, but was out with an injury for the 2023 event. That opened the door for Djokovic to win it for the third time. He also won his 23rd Grand Slam title, breaking a tie with Nadal for the most ever. Djokovic also took back the No. 1 ranking from Alcaraz.

The new all-time champ: Djokovic.

One of a Kind

At Wimbledon in July, **Carlos Alcaraz** exacted revenge for his French Open semifinals loss to **Novak Djokovic**. Alcaraz beat Djokovic in a grueling, five-set final to win Wimbledon for the first time.

It was Alcaraz's second career Grand Slam title, but his first with Djokovic in the field. It again made Alcaraz the No. 1 men's player. Even the old No. 1 agreed. "He's proven he's the best player in the world, no doubt," Djokovic said.

2023 MEN'S GRAND SLAMS

AUSTRALIAN OPEN	**Novak Djokovic**
FRENCH OPEN	**Novak Djokovic**
WIMBLEDON	**Carlos Alcaraz**
US OPEN	**Novak Djokovic**

At the Net: 2023

Pegula and the Buffalo Bills fell short.

Roller-Coaster Ride

The Australian Open in January 2023 featured highs and lows for American tennis star Jessica Pegula. Born in Buffalo, Pegula is a big Bills fan—and the daughter of the NFL team's owners Kim and Terry Pegula. The day before the Australian Open began, the Bills beat the Dolphins in an AFC Wild Card Playoff Game. Then Pegula won her first four matches in the tennis tournament.

Both runs came to an end, though. The Bills lost to the Bengals in a playoff game, and, two days later, the No. 3–seeded Pegula lost to No. 24 Victoria Azarenka of Belarus in the quarterfinals in Australia.

Bad News/Good News

First, the bad news: The Grand Slam drought for American men's tennis players continued through midsummer in 2023. No US player has won a singles title at a major since Andy Roddick won the US Open way back in 2003. Now the good news: The future for US men's tennis is looking bright. After the Australian Open, 10 Americans ranked among the top 50 in the ATP rankings. Nine were 25 or younger.

And Then There Was One

After Roger Federer announced his retirement in 2022, the Big Three that dominated men's tennis around the world for 20 years was down to two. Then Rafael Nadal announced that 2024 would be his final season. Nadal, the winner of 22 Grand Slam singles titles—a record until Novak Djokovic topped it in 2023—was forced to withdraw from the French Open in 2023 with a hip injury. At that time, he admitted that injuries had begun to take a toll on him. He decided then to sit out several months and make the 2024 season his last.

That will leave only Djokovic remaining from the Big Three. He'll be 37 in 2024, and he can't go on forever. Then again, the Serbian star has shown no signs of slowing down.

Hall of Famer Esther Vergeer.

Tennis Hall of Famers

Wheelchair tennis stars **Esther Vergeer** and **Rick Draney** formed the Class of 2023 at the International Tennis Hall of Fame. They were inducted in ceremonies in Newport, Rhode Island, in July.

Vergeer, who is from the Netherlands, was the No. 1–ranked player in the world for a staggering 668 weeks from 2000 to 2013. In one (very long!) stretch, she won an incredible 470 matches in a row. She won 21 Grand Slam singles titles and seven gold medals—four in singles and three in doubles—at the Paralympics.

Draney, an American, reached No. 1 in the rankings in both singles and doubles in the late 1990s. Just as important, he has been a pioneer in bringing the quad division (for athletes with additional restrictions in the playing arm) to tennis at the Paralympics and other tournaments.

MAJOR CHAMPIONS

Here are the men and women with the most Grand Slam singles titles in the Open Era (since 1968).

MEN'S GRAND SLAMS

PLAYER	TITLES
Novak **DJOKOVIC**	23
Rafael **NADAL**	22
Roger **FEDERER**	20
Pete **SAMPRAS**	14
Bjorn **BORG**	11

WOMEN'S GRAND SLAMS

PLAYER	TITLES
Serena **WILLIAMS**	23▶
Steffi **GRAF**	22
Chris **EVERT**	18
Martina **NAVRATILOVA**	18
Margaret **COURT**	11

OTHER SPORTS

THE NEW ALL-TIME CHAMP
With her 87th career World Cup ski race win, America's Mikaela Shiffrin set a new world record for men and women. She topped the mark of 86 set by Sweden's Ingemar Stenmark. A few weeks before, Shiffrin went past fellow American skier Lindsey Vonn's women's record of 82. For Shiffrin, the record was especially sweet. In the 2022 Winter Olympics, she shocked herself and the skiing world by going medal-less. But she was mentally tough enough to bounce back to her winning ways in 2023! For more on 2022–23 winter sports action, turn to page 176.

France's Pauline Bourdon did her best on this play, but New Zealand came out ahead.

Women's Rugby

Rugby is not super-popular in the United States, but it's beloved in many parts of the world. A fast, hard-hitting sport, it calls for athletes to be quick, tough, and smart. Also, rugby is one of the sports that is seeing a growing number of women play. How popular is it becoming? In November 2022, the Women's Rugby World Cup set an all-time attendance record for the final game, played in Auckland, New Zealand. The World Cup matched the top 16 teams in the world and featured some thrilling play.

SEMIFINALS

New Zealand 25, France 24

The home country almost went home early, but France missed a penalty kick late in the game. "I thought it was gone, but it wasn't gone," said New Zealand coach **Wayne Smith**. "It's there and we've got a chance next week." **Ruby Tui** and **Theresa Fitzpatrick** scored for the home side, while **Romane Ménager** had a pair for France.

England 26, Canada 19

Canada surprised England, who had won 25 games in a row, with a tough match. England pulled ahead early, but Canada came back to tie it 12-12. The game was close in the second half before England's **Abby Dow** raced to her second try (a score, like a touchdown in football) and Canada ran out of time.

42,579

The record attendance at the Women's World Cup final match at Eden Park in Auckland, New Zealand

CHAMPIONSHIP
New Zealand 34, England 31

The home fans went home happy as the Kiwis became the first host nation to win this World Cup. It was a back-and-forth thriller with great play on both sides. New Zealand found itself in a hole early, as England led 14-0 after only 15 minutes. However, England fell a player short after a red card. The Kiwis took advantage and both **Ayesha Leti-I'Iga** and **Amy Rule** had tries (worth five points each), but they trailed at halftime 26-19. In the second half, New Zealand thrilled the crowd with a go-ahead try by **Krystal Murray**. But England's "Red Roses" roared back, as **Amy Cokayne** scored her third try of the match to put England ahead. With just nine minutes left in the 80-minute game, Leti-I'iga pounded over to put New Zealand back on top. The locals held on against a desperate English attack to win and claim the Cup. As this chart of all-time champs shows, though, winning was nothing new for New Zealand: this was their sixth all-time championship!

All-Time Women's Rugby WORLD CUP CHAMPIONS

2022*	**New Zealand**
2017	**New Zealand**
2014	**England**
2010	**New Zealand**
2006	**New Zealand**
2002	**New Zealand**
1998	**New Zealand**
1994	**England**
1991	**United States**

*Held in 2022 due to a pandemic delay, this World Cup was officially the 2021 event.

New Zealand celebrated its World Cup wins in front of delighted home fans.

CHAMPIONS

Winter Sports

Shiffrin with her World Cup

SKIING

Along with breaking the world record for total race victories (page 172), American **Mikaela Shiffrin** won her fifth overall World Cup title, piling up nearly 1,000 points more than the second-place finisher. She was also the overall winner in slalom and giant slalom. Italy's **Sofia Goggia** was the downhill champ, while Switzerland's **Lara Gut-Behrami** won Super G. Another Swiss skier, **Marco Odermatt**, won his first overall championship. He was also tops in Super G and giant slalom. Two skiers from Norway also won titles: **Aleksandr Aamodt Kilde** in downhill and **Lucas Braathen** in slalom.

Marco Odermatt slalomed his way to the top.

US Figure Skating Championships

Nathan Chen had won six US men's singles titles in a row. But for the 2023 event, he was taking time off to finish college at Yale. That opened the door for an exciting young skater to leap to the top of the podium. Using a mix of amazing jumps and smooth skating, **Ilia Malinin** earned his first national title. The women's winner was also a first-timer: 15-year-old **Isabeau Levito**. She won both parts of the competition and nailed some difficult jumps in the free skate. **Alexa Knierim** and **Brandon Frazier** won the pairs title, while **Madison Chock** and **Evan Bates** were ice dance champs. Chock and Bates later won their first world championship, too!

Isabeau Levito

Sledding Sports

Some highlights of the 2023 competitions in bobsled, luge, and skeleton:

* American **Kaillie Humphries** (right) won her eighth bobsled medal (a bronze in two-woman), setting a new World Championships record.

* Germany and Italy dominated luge World Cup. German athletes won women's singles and men's doubles, while Italian lugers were men's singles and women's doubles champs. Germany broke the unofficial tie by winning the team relay.

* In skeleton (the headfirst sledding style), Germany's **Christopher Grotheer** was the men's champion. Another German, **Tina Hermann**, won the women's title.

Team USA at the World Games included more than 200 athletes from 46 states.

Special Olympics World Games

More than 6,500 athletes from around the world came to Berlin, Germany, to take part in more than 25 sports. The Special Olympics is for people with mental and developmental challenges. They train year-round with coaches, winning national events to earn a spot in the World Games. More than 190 countries sent athletes to Berlin. Here are some of the highlights of this awesome event!

She Can Do It All!

Loretta Claiborne of the US team is a modern-day **Babe Zaharias** (look her up; she was one of the best woman athletes ever!). Loretta won the singles tennis in Berlin, but winning was nothing new for her. She also won medals in past Games in running, bowling, and figure skating! Oh, and in Berlin, she was almost 70 years old! Other highlights of the US team included **Charlie Phillips** from Missouri, who earned four weightlifting medals, including silver in the men's all-around, and **Tyler Dodson**, who helped win a sailing medal even after his boat flipped over in one race.

Nothing Can Stop Him

Jamaica's **Kirk Wint** was born with both physical and mental disabilities. When he was young, his family could not afford a wheelchair, so he learned to walk—and run—using his hands and knees. In Berlin, Kirk returned to his third Special Olympics. He took part in the 50-meter run. In a previous Games, he was a winner in the softball throw.

Kirk Wint didn't let anything stop him!

Golden Splashes

Three athletes from India won swimming medals on the same day! **Prashaddhi K.** had two, while **Diksha S.** got another.

San Marino's Marianna Pruccoli

Madhav M. also picked up three silvers. (The Indian athletes only used their first name and initial.) Great Britain's **Taylor Mackenzie** also won a pair of golds.

Marvelous on the Mat

Two great stories came out of the gymnastics events. **Annabelle Tschech-Löffler** won a bronze in the beam for Germany. At 13, she was the youngest athlete in the event. Because the games were in Berlin, most of her family could join her celebration. The tiny nation of San Marino sent athletes, and while the country, surrounded by Italy, has never won an Olympic gold medal, **Marianna Pruccoli** earned Special Olympics gold in rhythmic gymnastics!

Soccer Champs

Special Olympians play seven-a-side soccer. In the men's event, dozens of teams battled for a week until the final match was set. Ireland took on Morocco and won 2-1. The celebration after the match was epic!

Mage (right) came out ahead after a furious final sprint in the Kentucky Derby.

2023 Triple Crown

The three most famous American horse races are known together as the Triple Crown. Winning all three is a mighty challenge for horse and rider. Since the first Kentucky Derby way back in 1875, the Triple Crown has been won only 13 times. The 2023 racing season did not add to that total, but fans still saw exciting races.

Kentucky Derby: Injuries knocked more horses out of the "Run for the Roses" than in any year since 1936. Sadly, some of those injuries were serious enough that the horses had to be put down. **Mage**, ridden by **Javier Castellano**, wound up the winner. The horse galloped into the lead on the race's final turn and sprinted home to win by a length.

Preakness Stakes: This race in Baltimore ended with a thrilling dash to the finish. At the wire, **National Treasure** and

John Velazquez nosed ahead of **Blazing Sevens** to win. Mage finished third, ending his Triple Crown hopes.

Belmont Stakes: This is the longest of the three races and held near New York City. The 2023 running made history. **Jena Antonucci** became the first woman to train a Triple Crown race winner. She watched **Arcangelo** speed across the finish line, guided by Castellano. It was his first Belmont Stakes win as well.

2023 Tour de France

Until stage 16 of the 2023 Tour de France, the famous cycling event was a two-man race. Denmark's **Jonas Vingegaard** and Slovenia's **Tadej Pogačar** were just seconds part. Both held the lead at different points, and fans were loving the back-and-forth action.

Then in stage 16, a time trial, Vingegaard gained almost a minute over his rival. The next day, the 155 remaining riders had to conquer a mountain! The ride up the Col de la Loze covered 155 miles, most of it uphill. Challenging mountain stages late in the race are very difficult, but Vingegaard treated it like an easy ride in the country. He roared out and ended up gaining almost six minutes over Pogačar. That was just too much of a lead to overcome, even though Pogačar did win a stage late in the race.

The Danish rider became the sixth cyclist to win back-to-back Tours de France. The top American finisher was **Sepp Kuss**, who was on Vingogaard's winning team, too.

A costumed fan chased Vingegaard!

Women's TDF

Though shorter in time and distance than the men's Tour de France, the women's edition is still a very tough race! Athletes have to pedal nearly 1,000 km (621 miles) in a week! In the next-to-last stage, **Demi Vollering** (left) of the Netherlands powered through a steep mountain climb to grab the overall lead. She held on during the final-day time trial to win her first Tour de France. **Lotte Kopecky** of Belgium had led most of the race but fell to second place.

Aspen Action!
Winter X Games

The high-flying, gravity-beating imaginations and skills of the world's best action sports stars landed in Aspen, Colorado, in January 2023. Here are some of the highlights.

Put a Cork In It

One of the hardest tricks in snowboarding had never been done by a female athlete until these X Games. Then three women pulled it off! **Anna Gasser** did one in practice. Then Japan's **Reira Iwabuchi** became the first to land one in an event, and it helped her win the Big Air gold medal. Canada's **Laurie Blouin** later matched the trick. So what was it? A frontside triple 1260, called a "cork."

Mark McMorris

Gaon Choi has the smile of a winner!

That means spinning three-and-a-half turns in the air before landing . . . on a snowboard!

Great Start!

At 14 years old, **Gaon Choi** of South Korea became the youngest Winter X Games medalist ever. She won the Superpipe competition with a series of jaw-dropping moves. She beat the age record of two-time Olympic gold medalist **Chloe Kim**, who helped Choi move from Korea to train in the US!

He's Number 1!

Canadian snowboarding legend **Mark McMorris** has been thrilling fans and judges for years as one of the sport's all-time greats. In Aspen, he earned gold in the Slopestyle event. That gave him 22 all-time golds at the Winter X Games, the most ever. He had to hold off double-gold medalist **Marcus Kleveland** to win.

SoCal Sunshine!
Summer X Games

After two years without fans, the Summer X Games bounced back in 2023 with a Southern California extravaganza. Events were held in late July in Los Angeles, San Diego, and Ventura. Here are some of the highlights!

Young Star

Gui Khury completed a rare Judo 900 (2.5 complete spins in the air) to win gold in the Skateboarding Big Air event. Not bad for a guy who is only 14! One of his opponents was 55-year-old skateboarding legend **Tony Hawk**!

Triple Crown

Kevin Peraza earned gold in BMX Street. That gave him a unique triple crown, to go with his golds in previous X Games in BMX Park and BMX Dirt.

Wonders from Down Under

Chloe Covell and **Arisa Trew** had long trips from their home in Australia to California, but it was worth it! Covell won Women's Skateboard Street. At 13, she's the youngest woman ever to win the event and also the first Aussie. Also 13, Trew was the champ in Women's Skateboard Vert. Trew later became the first woman ever with a pair of skateboard golds when she won Skateboard Park, too.

Flying Motorcycles!

Motorcycles are supposed to stay on the ground. Tell that to the high-flying riders in Moto X High Air. **Colby Raha** soared to a new all-time record height of 56 feet, three inches to win gold.

Back to the Top

Mariah Duran earned gold in the Women's Skateboard Park Best Trick event. It was her first victory since 2018.

Awesome skateboarding action from Covell

Women's Cricket T20 World Cup

To most American sports fans, cricket is an insect. But to billions of people around the world, cricket is a massive deal. In nations such as Australia, India, Pakistan, Great Britain, and South Africa, the ball-and-bat sport is followed very closely. Some forms of cricket can take five days (yes . . . days!) to complete. A shorter, quicker, and more fast-paced version called T20 takes about three hours. Watching T20 has helped create even more cricket fans—check out some highlights online, and you might become a fan, too.

In 2023, the Women's T20 Cricket World Cup was held in South Africa. Australia continued its dominance, winning the title for the sixth time. They had to beat the host of the tournament in front of a very pro–South Africa crowd. Australia batted first and scored 166 runs, mostly thanks to star **Beth Mooney**'s 44. When South Africa got its turn, Australia's bowlers (kind of like baseball pitchers) mostly shut them down. **Laura Wolvaardt** did her best for the home team, scoring 61, but it was not enough. The championship was the third in a row for Australia, too.

In 2024, the men's T20 will include some games played in the United States, so keep an eye out for them!

Beth Mooney

Lacrosse

National Lacrosse League

The same two teams ended up in the NLL championship series after another fast-paced indoor lacrosse season. The Colorado Mammoth had to knock off two higher-seeded teams in the playoffs to reach the final. Meanwhile, the top-seeded Buffalo Bandits had no trouble, outscoring playoff opponents 51-21 before meeting Colorado. Each team won a game in the Finals before a winner-take-all Game 3. Then Buffalo poured it on, winning 13-4. It was the Bandits' first NLL title since 2008 and fifth all-time.

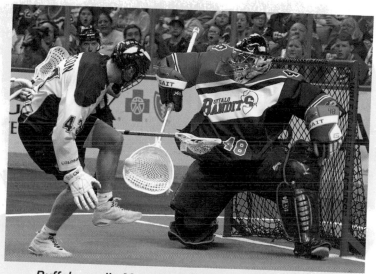

Buffalo goalie Matt Vinc comes up big in the final.

Premier Lacrosse League

The 2023 PLL regular season ended after we printed this book, but watch for this

Brennan O'Neill of Team USA

exciting outdoor league in 2024. Before the 2023 season started, the PLL held a Championship Series. In the final game, the Chrome held on to beat Atlas. Atlas led most of the way until **Justin Anderson** scored the go-ahead point with just a minute left in Chrome's 24-23 win.

World Lacrosse Championships

The best 14 outdoor teams in the world met in San Diego, and the US team came out on top for the second year in a row. They beat Canada 10-7 in the final match. MVP **Brennan O'Neill** had five of those goals to lead the way. A highlight was a third-place finish by the Haudenosaunee team, made up of Indigenous people from the US and Canada. Lacrosse was created by the Haudenosaunee hundreds of years ago!

CHAMPIONS!

NFL

GAME	SEASON	RESULT
LVII	2022	**Kansas City** 38, **Philadelphia** 35
LVI	2021	**L.A. Rams** 23, **Cincinnati** 20
LV	2020	**Tampa Bay** 31, **Kansas City** 9
LIV	2019	**Kansas City** 31, **San Francisco** 20
LIII	2018	**New England** 13, **L.A. Rams** 3
LII	2017	**Philadelphia** 41, **New England** 33
LI	2016	**New England** 34, **Atlanta** 28
50	2015	**Denver** 24, **Carolina** 10
XLIX	2014	**New England** 28, **Seattle** 24
XLVIII	2013	**Seattle** 43, **Denver** 8
XLVII	2012	**Baltimore** 34, **San Francisco** 31

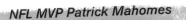

NFL MVP Patrick Mahomes

NFL MOST VALUABLE PLAYER

2022	**Patrick MAHOMES**, Kansas City
2021	**Aaron RODGERS**, Green Bay
2020	**Aaron RODGERS**, Green Bay
2019	**Lamar JACKSON**, Baltimore
2018	**Patrick MAHOMES**, Kansas City
2017	**Tom BRADY**, New England
2016	**Matt RYAN**, Atlanta
2015	**Cam NEWTON**, Carolina
2014	**Aaron RODGERS**, Green Bay
2013	**Peyton MANNING**, Denver

COLLEGE FOOTBALL

2022 **GEORGIA**		2016 **CLEMSON**
2021 **GEORGIA**		2015 **ALABAMA**
2020 **ALABAMA**		2014 **OHIO STATE**
2019 **LSU**		2013 **FLORIDA ST.**
2018 **CLEMSON**		2012 **ALABAMA**
2017 **ALABAMA**		2011 **ALABAMA**

Here's a handy guide to recent winners and champions of most of the major sports. They've all been celebrated in past editions of the YEAR IN SPORTS. But here they are all together again!

MLB

2022 Houston **ASTROS** 4, Philadelphia **PHILLIES** 2
2021 Atlanta **BRAVES** 4, Houston **ASTROS** 2
2020 Los Angeles **DODGERS** 4, Tampa Bay **RAYS** 2
2019 Washington **NATIONALS** 4, Houston **ASTROS** 3
2018 Boston **RED SOX** 4, Los Angeles **DODGERS** 1
2017 Houston **ASTROS** 4, Los Angeles **DODGERS** 3
2016 Chicago **CUBS** 4, Cleveland **INDIANS** 3
2015 Kansas City **ROYALS** 4, New York **METS** 1
2014 San Francisco **GIANTS** 4, Kansas City **ROYALS** 3
2013 Boston **RED SOX** 4, St. Louis **CARDINALS** 2
2012 San Francisco **GIANTS** 4, Detroit **TIGERS** 0

MLB MOST VALUABLE PLAYER

	AL	NL
2022	AARON **JUDGE**	PAUL **GOLDSCHMIDT**
2021	SHOHEI **OHTANI**	BRYCE **HARPER**
2020	JOSÉ **ABREU**	FREDDIE **FREEMAN**
2019	MIKE **TROUT**	CODY **BELLINGER**
2018	MOOKIE **BETTS**	CHRISTIAN **YELICH**
2017	JOSÉ **ALTUVE**	GIANCARLO **STANTON**
2016	MIKE **TROUT**	KRIS **BRYANT**
2015	JOSH **DONALDSON**	BRYCE **HARPER**
2014	MIKE **TROUT**	CLAYTON **KERSHAW**
2013	MIGUEL **CABRERA**	ANDREW **MCCUTCHEN**

COLLEGE BASKETBALL

YEAR	MEN'S	WOMEN'S
2023	Connecticut	LSU
2022	Kansas	S. Carolina
2021	Baylor	Stanford
2020	Not played	Not played
2019	Virginia	Baylor
2018	Villanova	Notre Dame
2017	N. Carolina	S. Carolina
2016	Villanova	Connecticut
2015	Duke	Connecticut
2014	Connecticut	Connecticut
2013	Louisville	Connecticut
2012	Kentucky	Baylor

NHL

2023	**Golden Knights** 4, Panthers 1
2022	**Avalanche** 4, Lightning 2
2021	**Lightning** 4, Canadiens 1
2020	**Lightning** 4, Stars 2
2019	**Blues** 4, Bruins 3
2018	**Capitals** 4, Golden Knights 1
2017	**Penguins** 4, Predators 2
2016	**Penguins** 4, Sharks 2
2015	**Blackhawks** 4, Lightning 2
2014	**Kings** 4, Rangers 1
2013	**Blackhawks** 4, Bruins 2

2022 WNBA champs: Las Vegas Aces

NBA

2023 **Denver Nuggets**
2022 **Golden State Warriors**
2021 **Milwaukee Bucks**
2020 **Los Angeles Lakers**
2019 **Toronto Raptors**
2018 **Golden State Warriors**
2017 **Golden State Warriors**
2016 **Cleveland Cavaliers**
2015 **Golden State Warriors**
2014 **San Antonio Spurs**
2013 **Miami Heat**

WNBA

2023 _____
2022 **Las Vegas Aces**
2021 **Chicago Sky**
2020 **Seattle Storm**
2019 **Washington Mystics**
2018 **Seattle Storm**
2017 **Minnesota Lynx**
2016 **Los Angeles Sparks**
2015 **Minnesota Lynx**
2014 **Phoenix Mercury**
2013 **Minnesota Lynx**

MLS

2022 **LAFC**

2021 **New York City FC**

2020 **Columbus Crew**

2019 **Seattle Sounders FC**

2018 **Atlanta United**

2017 **Toronto FC**

2016 **Seattle Sounders FC**

2015 **Portland Timbers**

NWSL

2022 **Portland Thorns FC**

2021 **Washington Spirit**

2020 **Canceled**

2019 **North Carolina Courage**

2018 **North Carolina Courage**

2017 **Portland Thorns FC**

2016 **Western New York Flash**

2015 **FC Kansas City**

FIFA WORLD PLAYER OF THE YEAR*

Year	Men	Women
2022	Lionel **Messi**	Alexia **Putellas**
2021	Robert **Lewandowski**	Alexia **Putellas**
2020	Robert **Lewandowski**	Lucy **Bronze**
2019	Lionel **Messi**	Megan **Rapinoe**#
2018	Luka **Modrić**	**Marta**
2017	Cristiano **Ronaldo**	Lieke **Martens**
2016	Cristiano **Ronaldo**	Carli **Lloyd**#
2015	Lionel **Messi**	Carli **Lloyd**#
2014	Cristiano **Ronaldo**	Nadine **Kessler**
2013	Cristiano **Ronaldo**	Nadine **Angerer**

* was known as the FIFA Ballon d'Or [Golden Ball] from 2010 to 2015.   # from the United States

PGA PLAYER OF THE YEAR

2022	Scottie **Scheffler**
2021	Patrick **Cantlay**
2020	Dustin **Johnson**
2019	Rory **McIlroy**
2018	Brooks **Koepka**
2017	Justin **Thomas**
2016	Dustin **Johnson**
2015	Jordan **Spieth**
2014	Rory **McIlroy**
2013	Tiger **Woods**
2012	Rory **McIlroy**

LPGA PLAYER OF THE YEAR

2022	Lydia **Ko**
2021	Jin Young **Ko**
2020	Sei Young **Kim**
2019	Jin Young **Ko**
2018	Ariya **Jutanugarn**
2017	Sung Hyun **Park** and So Yeon **Ryu**
2016	Ariya **Jutanugarn**
2015	Lydia **Ko**
2014	Stacy **Lewis**
2013	Inbee **Park**
2012	Stacy **Lewis**

ATP PLAYER OF THE YEAR

2022	Carlos **ALCARAZ**
2021	Novak **DJOKOVIC**
2020	Novak **DJOKOVIC**
2019	Rafael **NADAL**
2018	Novak **DJOKOVIC**
2017	Rafael **NADAL**
2016	Andy **MURRAY**
2015	Novak **DJOKOVIC**
2014	Novak **DJOKOVIC**
2013	Rafael **NADAL**
2012	Novak **DJOKOVIC**

WTA PLAYER OF THE YEAR

2022	Iga **ŚWIĄTEK**
2021	Ashleigh **BARTY**
2020	Sofia **KENIN**
2019	Ashleigh **BARTY**
2018	Simona **HALEP**
2017	Garbiñe **MUGURUZA**
2016	Angelique **KERBER**
2015	Serena **WILLIAMS**
2014	Serena **WILLIAMS**
2013	Serena **WILLIAMS**
2012	Serena **WILLIAMS**